Rachelle Allen
December 19, 2022

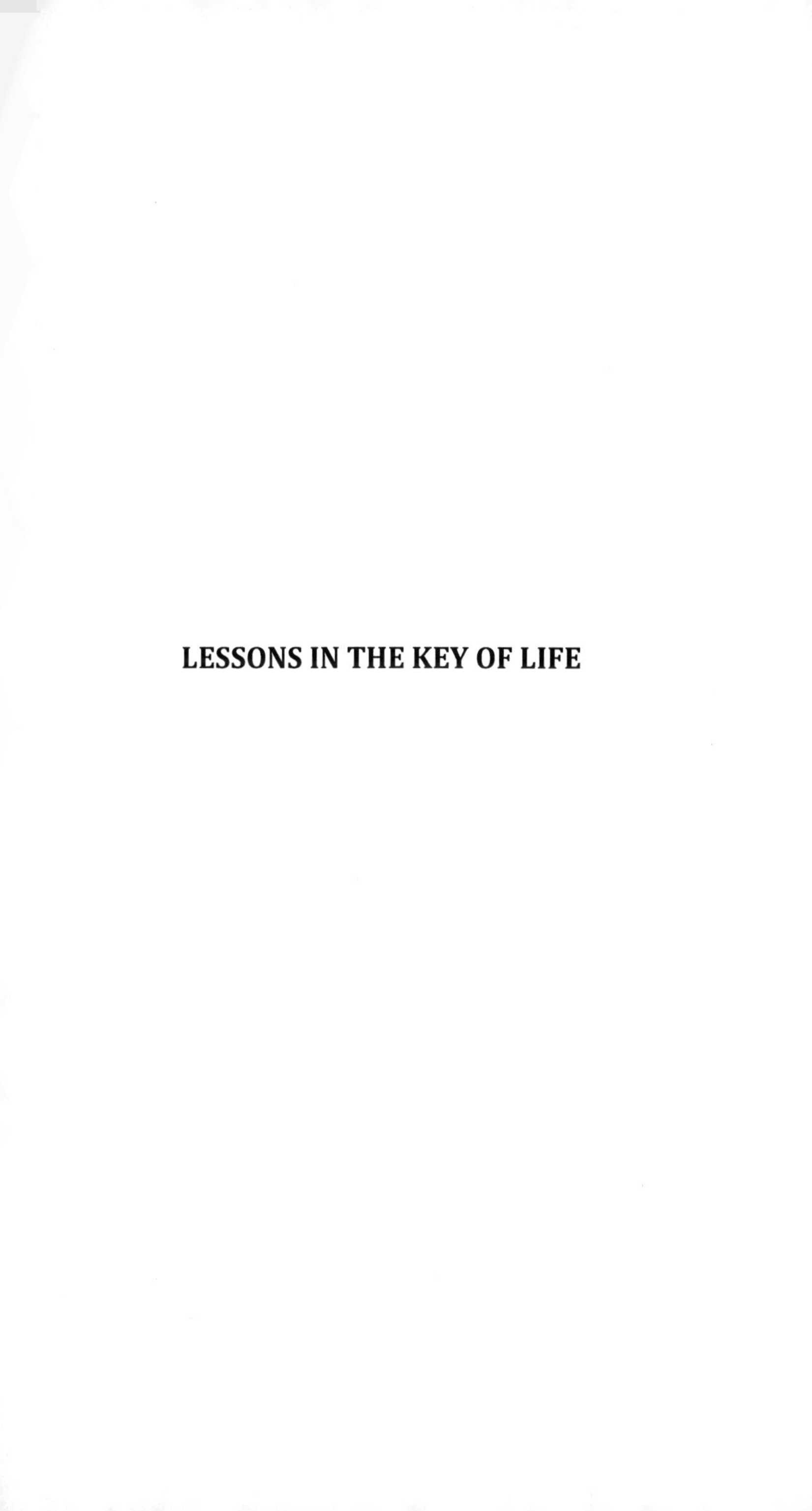

LESSONS IN THE KEY OF LIFE

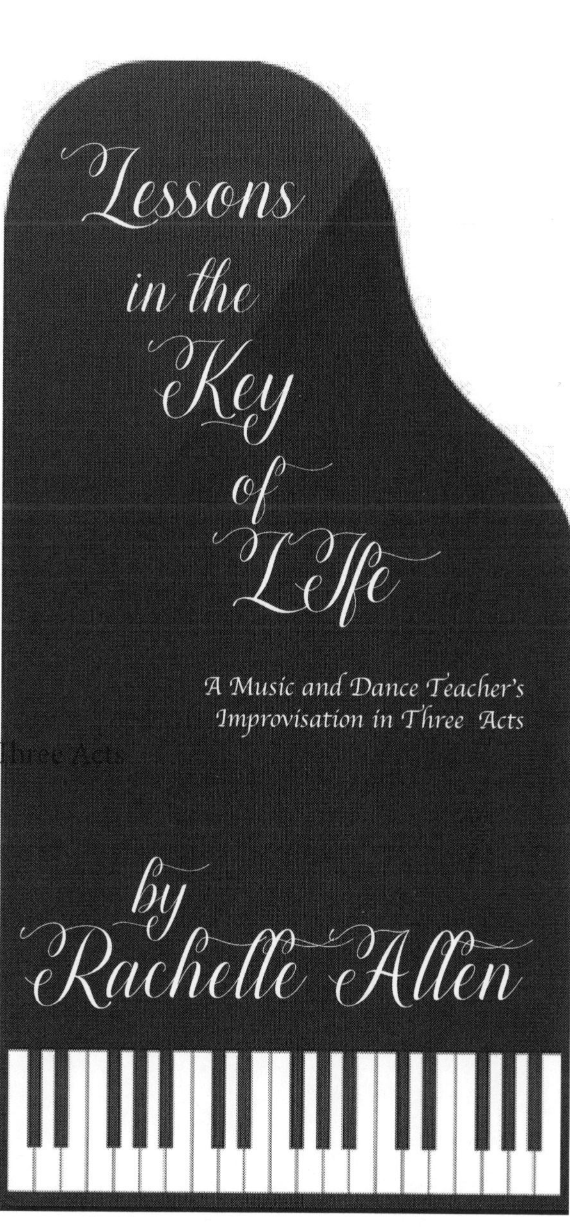
Lessons in the Key of Life
A Music and Dance Teacher's
Improvisation in Three Acts
by
Rachelle Allen

Lessons in the Key of Life
by
Rachelle Allen

A Pascal Editions Book
July 2022

First Edition Published by
Pascal Editions
Rochester New York

Layout and Cover Design by Pascal Editions

All names in this volume, with the exception of the Author, Anne Blauvelt, and those named in the Acknowledgments, have been changed to protect the privacy of the individuals mentioned.

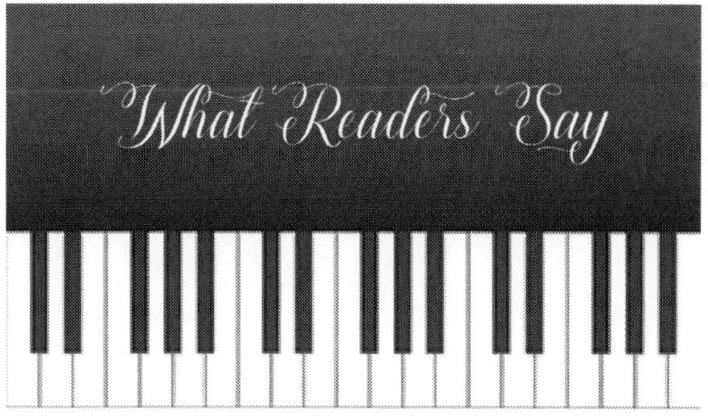

"I thoroughly enjoyed reading Rachelle's book. She shared much of her childhood days learning piano, singing, ballet, and even now, in later years, she had to learn to tap dance in a few short weeks. The book is filled with incredibly funny stories of her times teaching, and some, not so funny. But what I did find inspirational was the way she took on board each task she encountered and turned it into a lesson learned. All her love of teaching shines through each page. It was a pleasure to read."

- Sandra Stoner-Mitchell,
Author of the *Hedgerow Capers* series, *Eric and the Aliens, Beyond That Time*, and *The Witch and the Fairy*

"Heart-warming, insightful and often

down-right hilarious, Rachelle Allen's reflections on her career as a music and dance teacher is a must-read for anyone who has taught, been taught, or plans to teach. With words that dance and sing across the page, Shelley, as she's known to her students, imparts life-lessons inspired by decades of teaching students of all ages.

"By the end of the book, readers will be on their feet cheering for another encore!"

- Jenny Giessler,
Former Coordinator
Generation Two

"The joy that Shelley brings to her piano lessons resonates through this book. It is inspirational, funny, and thoroughly entertaining."

- Patricia Somerville, *M.D.*

"*Lessons in the Key of Life* is an extremely powerful story about the journey of teaching music. I was captivated by the story from start to finish as the life lessons included were invaluable and provided profound insight to one's everyday life.

"I will treasure what I learned in this book

and be mindful of the life teachings that were given as I apply these experiences to my daily life."

- Tamara Khalil
University of Maryland, Class of 2022

"Shelley's stories are both hilarious and poignant, written with the same keen eye, sharp wit, boundless creativity and tremendous heart that she brings to each one of her students' lessons each week. *Lessons in the Key of Life* captures what her piano families come to realize over time: that it has all been about so much more than piano lessons. That somehow, almost unwittingly, we find that the experience of making music each week has infused our lives with glimpses of what is most important. This gift is what makes both Shelley and her book of essays one of a kind."

- Laurie Couch
Adjunct English Professor,
Higher Education Enrollment professional

To my father, Bill Saxman, who nurtured the musician he saw in me early on, then kept me on a sensible path when I began to develop unreasonable stars in my eyes.

And to my exceptional educators, Lilene Berdy and Ann M. Blauvelt, who, by their loving examples, made me the teacher I am proud to be today.

Table of Contents

Summer Gigs

ACT THREE: Teaching Future Teachers to Teach

by

Anne Blauvelt

In 1982, I was teaching Kindergarten at the Penfield Village Nursery School and Kindergarten in Penfield, New York. One morning, I received a call from our Director, asking me to interview a young woman who wanted to volunteer at our school. That was the day that I met Rachelle Allen. I welcomed the opportunity to have help in my classroom and asked Rachelle why she wanted to volunteer. She told me that, because she was expecting her first child, she wanted to know how children learn.

As we worked together in the classroom,

I found Rachelle to be a natural teacher. I appreciated her warmth with the children and her sense of humor. We shared many laughs over the antics of our class of five–year-olds. I also learned about Rachelle's love of music. She plays the piano and flute and has a beautiful singing voice.

Since our time together in the classroom, Rachelle and I have become extremely close. She has, in fact, become like a very dear daughter.

In 1992, Rachelle began teaching piano, voice and flute to hundreds of children and many adults. Each year, her recitals demonstrate her students' accomplishments, and, occasionally, she delights the audience by performing with her students.

Lessons in the Key of Life is an enjoyable look at her life and career. I thoroughly enjoyed it, and I know that everyone who reads it will, as well.

Ann M. Blauvelt
Retired Teacher
Speaker on Kindergarten Readiness

Overture

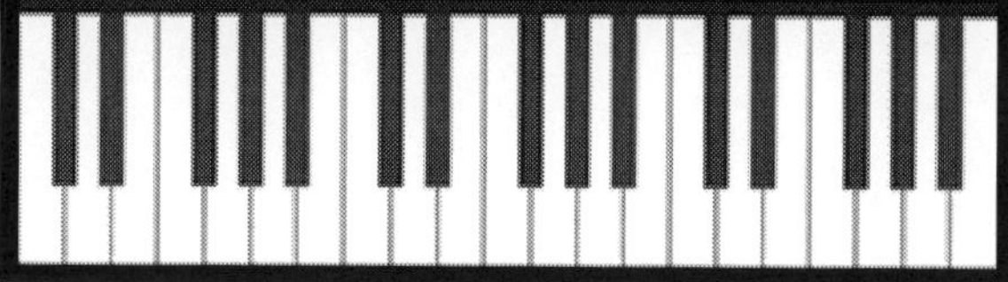

I invented my job – sort of. I'm an itinerant voice, flute, and piano teacher with seventy-three stops to make in a week. Although that sounds, even to me, rather over-the-top, the lesson-to-lesson pace of it, broken down into thirty-minute increments over six days, is not really all that taxing. In fact, it's as enjoyable as life gets. I especially like that no two days are ever the same. Still, that's not to say that mine is a stress-free existence. Some of the houses and families I visit would give The Addams Family a moment's pause. But, overall, it's fun and fulfilling and fits my personality with the perfection of a Vera Wang gown.

I remember with crystal clarity the day I "became" a teacher, and it had nothing at all to do with my graduation date. I was twenty-five, married, pregnant, and volunteering in a private kindergarten, working with a Master Teacher named Ann, who'd begun her career the year I was born.

Among her wards in this class of eight boys and two girls was five-year-old Jesse, doe-eyed, sentient, dear and brilliant. He was also done being good at 11:00 a.m. every day. It certainly wasn't that he wanted to misbehave or act out on a daily basis. He was simply "young" for his chronological age and, more than likely, often in need of a nap.

He loved the patriarch of our class's mouse family, a burly, active rodent named "Big Brownie." The minute we announced each day, "It's free time," Jesse was at the dry aquarium scooping his friend up for another shared frolic. One hard-and-fast rule in the room, though, was no mice in the wooden block corner. (Solid planks of wood up high versus small, furry, nearly weightless bodies below seemed a situation well worth avoiding.)

On this day, during free time, the class was busy with easel drawings, board games and wooden block skyscrapers when, as occurred on a daily basis, one of the elaborate block creations came careening to the floor. This time, though, the crash was followed by a chilling scream from Jesse. Ann and I watched him run toward us, carrying a furry lump on his outstretched hand. "I don't want to play with Big Brownie anymore!" he wailed. "He doesn't move!" Teeny beads of blood formed at the corner of Brownie's mouth, and his little rib cage was rising and falling at lightning speed.

"We're going to put him in his house for awhile," I told Jesse, "but he'll be fine."

Ann took me aside and said, "I don't think you should have said that, Rachelle. Now, when Big Brownie dies, Jesse's going to be even more upset."

"Ann," I said, "I grew up in the country, in a house surrounded by fifty-two acres of fields. One thing I know for sure is that, if you don't kill a rodent on contact, it springs back to life in no time."

Sure enough, by morning's end, Big Brownie was running around full speed on his little exercise wheel. But, in the meantime, kind-hearted, deep Jesse was out of his skin with the realization of what he'd done. He understood, all on his own, that his disobeying the rule had brought pain and fear to his beloved friend. With unbridled fury, he took one arm and swiped the length of a long shelf of toys, catapulting them in every direction as his classmates ran for cover. He then performed a like maneuver on the shelf below.

"Rachelle," Ann asked, "could you please take over the class?" She put a firm, gentle hand on each of her beloved Jesse's shoulders and headed him toward the book corner, while the rest of the class and I restored order to our room. Ann lay on her stomach with Jesse in the book corner, her arm around his waist, his head nestled into her collarbone. There they stayed, reading book after book, until this sweet boy, with the dearest of hearts and the poor judgment to which all children are entitled, was able to re-calibrate.

I watched with awe and realized, at once, that I had been given the gift of a lifetime to be able to witness something this special. I knew that, in the hands of a lesser teacher, this darling child's entire attitude toward school could have been changed forever. A lesser teacher would have said, in a sharp voice, "Jesse! Isn't it bad enough that you nearly killed Big Brownie by having him in the block corner when you knew you weren't supposed to? Now you're going to have a tantrum and make a mess of our room? What's wrong with you? Why are you behaving so badly? You go sit in the time-out chair until you can settle down!"

But Ann knew better. She knew this child, and she loved him, warts and all. And he went home that day with his self-esteem intact because she always practiced what she preached – the most sacred lesson I ever learned and the one I've lived by ever since.

Lesson:

The children who "deserve" your love the least are the ones who need it the most. (And it applies to grown-ups, too.)

1

My Own Piano Lesson Experience

My grandmother died when I was five, leaving my mother an inheritance substantial enough for the purchase of a full-length mink coat for herself, with enough left over for a Wurlitzer spinet piano for me (on substantial markdown because it had only eighty-six keys instead of eighty-eight).

Glory Days

I began lessons with Mrs. Brenner, a peppy, smiling woman so kind and nice that, during recess at school, whenever I played house, I became her. I was always Beverly, beautiful and nice to everyone.

Unlike the other children in our teeny town in 1961, and long before it became as common as it is today, I lived in a two-career family. Both my parents worked not only outside of our rural home, but twenty-five miles away in what everyone I knew referred to as "The City." And, because all our relatives lived hours away, they arranged for me to go to a babysitter's before and after school each day.

My new caregiver was a scowly-faced woman with an unpredictable love of yelling. In her dark and foreboding living room sat a huge, old upright piano with keys like a set of decaying dentures. None of her teenagers ever touched it, so I had carte blanche to practice on it every single day.

In no time, I discovered that none of her other wards – a sweet brother and sister whose mom had died, a whiny girl from next door with stringy hair, and even the babysitter's mean, sneaky, six-year-old daughter – was allowed to disturb me when I was at the piano. I noticed, too, that as long as I was playing, my babysitter seemed a lot happier. Many days, she even hummed along from the kitchen. She never said so, but I always wondered if the piano had been hers at my age, because they both seemed so old. (You know, like thirty.)

The school bus dropped me off there at 3:30 p.m. every day, and my father arrived to retrieve me at 5:15. Needless to say, with nearly two hours of practice five days each week, I excelled at piano quickly. I lived for my Saturday piano lesson time, when I could show Beverly Brenner all my newfound skills. She was crazy about me!

Lesson:

Even a skill you acquire under duress
is still one you get to keep forever
and use to your advantage.

Dark Days

In third grade, though, Mrs. Brenner's husband found a much better job in Philadelphia and took her away from me. I felt bereft. Also that year, my mother announced that I would be going to a different babysitter's before and after school. (In our house, elaborate communication was a lost art. Parents gave directions, and offspring followed them. It was a simple, efficient operation.) The new babysitter turned out to be even scowlier-faced than the first. She also yelled substantially more, and, worst of all, had no piano. Not that it mattered, really, since I no longer had a piano teacher.

Thankfully, I began flute lessons at school that year, so that filled my musical void to a satisfactory degree. Since I could already read music, this new instrument came easily to me. I absolutely loved the sound of it, and I practiced constantly. Like Mrs. Brenner, my band teacher praised me often.

The week before fourth grade began, I heard my mother lament to my babysitter that she wished she could find another piano teacher for me because I just didn't seem as happy since Beverly Brenner left. That afternoon, my babysitter mentioned to my father that the husband and wife who lived next door were piano professors at the internationally acclaimed music school in The City and that, if he wanted, she could ask them if I could take lessons with them.

My mother looked elated, but I could tell by his expression that my father wasn't sold on the idea. He said he'd run into them several times at my babysitter's house when he was picking me up and found them to be pompous and stuffy. I wasn't sure exactly what that meant, but gathered it wasn't a particularly ringing endorsement.

Nonetheless, my mother's enthusiasm won out, and lessons began. In no time at all, the meaning of "pompous" and "stuffy" became painfully clear to me.

"Are those the clothes you actually wore to school today, Dear?" the husband asked me one day.

"No, these are my play clothes," I answered.

"Play clothes?" he repeated with a sneer. "Where do you play? At the town dump?"

That gave him and his wife a really good chuckle.

Another time, he said, "You are very thin and pale." That made his wife ask, "Does your family feed you enough?"

I always felt like Oliver Twist at their house. Plus, I could never please them musically either. Whatever I played was never fast/slow/loud/quiet/smooth/detached "enough." It seemed to me as if they were never even remotely satisfied with my work the entire time I studied with them. I left their house each week feeling like the stupidest, most inept student on the planet.

I spent two grueling years with these people, never once complaining about them to my parents. Stoicism was a highly prized commodity in our house, and I felt convinced that saying my feelings were being hurt every week was not going to be a good enough reason, in my parents' eyes, for me to be allowed to quit. Of course, seeing this now, from an adult's standpoint, I know how misguided that thinking was.

I cried myself to sleep so many nights for the loss of my beloved Beverly Brenner, who had found me brilliant and stoked my talent.

The last straw was the day the husband chided, in his ever-patronizing, highly sarcastic way, "Well, as long as you're being barbaric enough to chew gum during your piano lesson, the least you could do is chomp it on the beat." That was "It" for me. Barbaric? I played two instruments, took ballet lessons every week, and was a Junior Girl Scout in good standing. Barbaric, my ass!

I stopped practicing from that lesson on because the piano seemed joyless to me now, and pleasing that man was the very last thing I ever wanted to do.

So the next week, when my mother reminded me, before leaving for my babysitter's, that I needed to take my piano books for my lesson that day, I glowered at her, yanked them off the piano, threw them to the floor, and screamed, "I am NOT taking piano lessons anymore, and I do not care what you say or what you do to me! I. AM. THROUGH!"

The woman was absolutely flabbergasted. I was the youngest of her four children by twelve years. I was quiet, conscientious, obedient, excellent in school and, unbegrudgingly, everyone's favorite. Yet, without warning, here I was being defiant in epic proportion.

"You have to finish out the year," she said, still visibly shaken. I immediately did the math: four more weeks of torture.

"I'M NOT DOING IT!" I screamed at her and, to my amazement, with no subsequent discussion on the matter, she conceded.

Lesson:

It is not brave to endure perpetual derision and pain. With as many life-affirming alternatives as there are in the world, it is both unnecessary and foolish.

Victorious Days

The following September, I began junior high and, after several phone calls to the school, my mother learned that the wife of the new band teacher from Boston taught piano. "You'll be taking lessons from her," my mother informed me. And because I missed playing so much, I decided that I would be willing to follow parental directions once again.

My new teacher wasn't Beverly Brenner – no one ever would be – but she was kind at all times, even when I gave practicing a low priority to my burgeoning adolescent social life. She never stopped expecting me to be excellent, or showing me how to achieve that status as she went over fingerings with me, provided reams of music theory pages to complete each week, and challenged me with piece after piece that seemed impossible to master. But when it came time to audition for college, I tested out of the first two years' worth of piano pedagogy and received a hefty scholarship, the only Vocal Performance Major / Piano Minor to have done so in years, I was told by the head of the department.

Lesson:

When teaching is cultivated with encouragement, understanding, and high-but-achievable expectations, there is no end to the blossoming it can render.

2

Father Knows Best

When I was fifteen years old, I implored my father, "Please, please, Daddy; I've been taking piano lessons for ten years. Can't I stop now so I can concentrate on just voice?"

"I'm sorry," he said, without a moment's hesitation, "that is not an option for you. Singers are a dime a dozen, but a singer who can play piano with the same expertise that she can sing has a chance for a career in music."

At that moment, and for quite awhile afterward, I was absolutely furious with that man! Why, oh why, was he insisting I suffer so?

But then, when I began teaching, and my roster of students grew, I could not ignore the fact that only a small percentage of my sweeties were vocalists. All the rest were learning to play piano.

Lesson:

Like my father, parents should have faith
in the vision of The Big Picture,
knowing that, sometimes, it is necessary
to make their offspring unhappy
in the short term, in order for it
to lead to something more positive
in the years to come.

3

Living The Dream

After leaving college, I had to have a tonsillectomy, every vocalist's nightmare. During the year afterward, when my voice was healing and I was not allowed to sing, I attended paralegal school as sort of a Plan B in case my voice never did return, and fame and fortune eluded me. Certainly, I wasn't about to merely teach piano! I was, after all, an aspiring operatic soprano with star quality!

In the afternoons, after paralegal classes were over, my vast talent and I waited tables at a nearby restaurant. My father referred to it as "a lesson in humility," adding, "... something you could sorely use." Hmpf!

Finally, though, my voice healed, and I resumed lessons with the same beloved voice teacher I'd had since eighth grade, a well-known NYC opera diva herself, who eventually got me the contact I needed to land an audition for the chorus of a big opera company in Manhattan. I was out of my skin with excitement when I received word that I'd been hired for the gig.

The pay was not great, however, so I subsidized the paltry wages by becoming a rehearsal pianist for various Off-off-off Broadway (think "New Jersey") shows.

At one particular audition for such a gig, the show's musical director, a greasy-haired, blubbery-lipped man with Coke-bottle glasses and a shirt mottled with remnants of his lunch, placed his doughy hand upon my thigh and commented on what a great rehearsal "team" we could make. The way I described the encounter that evening on the phone with my father was, "He may have been talking pianos, but he was thinking organs."

"That's it. You're coming home!" my father said at once.

"I'm not coming home," I insisted. "I haven't even been here a month yet. I'm going to become a famous opera star. That has always been my goal, and I'm going to make it happen. I'm a big girl. I can handle myself."

But, as the months went on, my struggling-artist lifestyle began to take its toll. Money was tight, so luxuries were few, and the perpetual honking and wheezing of the city traffic wreaked havoc with my countrified sleeping patterns and musician's ears. Plus, my two paying gigs each day left me feeling frustrated and unfulfilled.

At opera chorus rehearsals, my assignment was to be the human equivalent of a packing peanut: soften the impact of a precious commodity (the principal) against the harshness of his or her surroundings (the gargantuan stage). Limited movement, limited singing, understated everything. Always think as a group. Refrain from standing out. Less is not just more; it's all you're hired to give.

At rehearsals where I accompanied for Off-Broadway shows, Job One was to follow the vocalists. When they lost pitch, it was incumbent upon me to help them find it again or, occasionally, when that was simply not going to happen, to play in the key toward which they were skittering closest. If they wanted to slow the tempo through a measure or two (or six) and then, without warning, catapult through the next dozen, I was the musical equivalent of Mama Bunny to their recalcitrant Runaway Bunny, saying, in essence, with my instrument, "If you run away, I will run after you, for you are my little bunny!"

Somehow, covering for sub-par vocalists didn't seem like what an aspiring operatic soprano should be doing as her ongoing daily gig.

Finally, one Friday night, half a year later, after a particularly ego-deflating week, I called home, beleaguered, and asked my father, "Why would I be given a talent like this if I weren't going to also be given the personality I need to accommodate it?"

"That," said my father wisely, "is what you'll have to figure out with your life. That's the path to your happiness."

So, very soon afterward, I returned to my town of origin to begin the discovery process.

Lesson:

If you try on a dream for size
and discover it doesn't fit
the way it should,
you get to exchange it for Wisdom
and something substantially more
to your liking.

Act One

Dancing

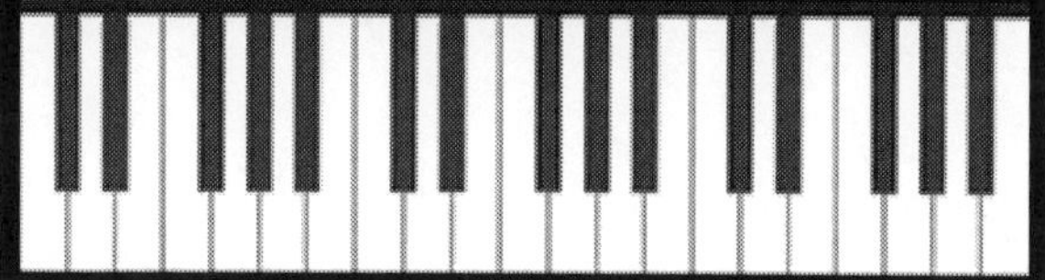

Within a month of returning home,
I moved to The City,
where, in time, marriage, motherhood,
and many unexpected career twists
followed.

4

Winging It

One Friday night, during services at my synagogue, I sat behind the writer and director of the Men's Club Variety Show. He introduced himself to me afterward, told me my voice was beautiful, and asked if I'd be willing to participate in his upcoming production.

At the first rehearsal, he questioned the cast, "Can anybody here dance?" I raised my hand politely, recalling my formative years at the Marion Sunderville School of Ballet, as well as my times choreographing routines at college for our sixteen-person swing choir. But then I noticed mine was the only arm aloft.

"Think you could work up a few routines to go along with skits I've written, and teach them to the cast?" he asked with hopeful eyebrows raised.

"Sure," I smiled. "No problem."

He proceeded to assign me several routines, one of which stood out from all the others: his Borscht Belt rendition of "Swan Lake."

The lead was a sixty-something, bespectacled woman named Golda. Her prince, Sollie, was a stout, silver-haired, retired office-supplies salesman with a perpetual smile and the comedic timing of Jerry Seinfeld. "I square dance every Saturday night," Sollie confided to me with an impish grin. "Ballet is going to be a new adventure. It is, though, I assure you," he said with a slight bow, "one I am very much looking forward to learning."

The back-up dancer swans were eight men, all over sixty, at various stages of hair loss and waistline gain, but twinkly-eyed and full of mirth, mischief and charm. They worked doggedly at every rehearsal and never once complained. By our fourth week, these people were so good that I invited our director and the handful of cast members working on a skit in the next room to come take a look.

The sight-gag of how completely un-swanlike these ten people were was uproarious. Little wren-like Golda and her gaggle of large ostrichesque men doing tongue-in cheek, serious-faced arabesques and pirouettes, all ramrod straight, all on the beat, and all perfectly synchronized, was schtick at its absolute finest. And, when dress rehearsal arrived, everything got even better.

On their tippy toes, in big, brown work boots, my swans tramped onto the stage at break-neck speed, swaddled in white thermal onesies that were embellished from the waist down with cascades of frothy white tuille.

Golda came on in what surely must have been a bridesmaid dress from the 60's – hot pink, shiny, foofy, and now shortened to the knees. It was accessorized with a pair of hot pink, sparkly gladiator sandals. Sollie bounded forth in tights, a flannel nightshirt in Tartan plaid, and a feathered, tri-cornered hat.

I've been in countless productions throughout the years, but this one was, by far, the most enjoyable, no close seconds.

Lesson:

Dignity is highly overrated.
If performing isn't fun,
then why is anyone bothering?

5

Opportunity Knocks

During rehearsal breaks for the Men's Club Variety Show, I put my time to good use by cutting the materials I was going to need the next day at the school where I had met my mentor, Ann. I was on their sub list by now, and often would be called in to work.

One night, a woman I recognized as a cast member from the "Perfecting Machine" sketch asked me why I was making dinosaurs, and I explained about the gig awaiting me in the morning.

"Would you be willing to be on the sub list at the JCC, the Jewish Community Center, too?" she asked with raised eyebrows and an enthusiastic smile. "I'm in charge of the Early Childhood department, and I'm always looking for good teachers. I figure anyone who can work the miracles you did with Sollie and Golda and those swans has got to be extraordinary!"

Two days later, they called me to sub there for a twelve-day tour. Another month after that, the pre-school dance teacher resigned, and I accepted the offered position.

Lesson:

Teaching is also a "performing art"
and, as such, requires
talent and creativity,
dedication and hard work,
which does not go unnoticed
by those in the field.

6

This Time, Opportunity Taps

The dance studio at the JCC was outstanding: enormous, with a gleaming hardwood floor. One wall hosted a floor-to-ceiling window, another a floor-to-ceiling mirror, and the last, two dance barres – a high one for adults, a lower one for children – running the entire length of the studio. Nothing I'd ever been in, even in Manhattan, compared. If only Miss Marion were here to see where her training had taken me!

Just before the new year, however, I was advised that renovations were going to begin soon and, thus, foot traffic would be re-routed through the dance studio. My classes would have to held in one of the auditoriums for a while.

At the end of the second week, I found a note in my mailbox in the Early Childhood department: "Shelley, Please come to my office. We need to talk. Rose Melnick."

("Shelley" is what I was always called as a child, though my mother's version of it was a little different. I believe I was twelve before I realized my named wasn't really Larry–Linda–Donna–SHELLEY! But since everyone in the Jewish community knew me when I was little, "Shelley" is the moniker they continued to use. Too bad for me if, after earning my degrees, I wanted to seem all grown up and reclaim my given name, Rachelle. At the JCC, I was, and would always be, "Shelley.")

But back to Rose Melnick.

My heart thumped like the bass drum in an Army band, and perspiration formed on my face and neck. Although I didn't know exactly what Rose Melnick's position was at the JCC, I did know she had a secretary and a private office, and was definitely one of the Powers That Be. I also knew her note sounded ominous, and that I suddenly felt very sick to my stomach.

I swallowed down my fear and knocked on her half-opened door unannounced, since her secretary was out.

"Oh, Shelley! Come in!" She waved a gesture of invitation. "Close the door, though, will you please?"

My stomach lurched.

"Sit down," she coaxed.

I did as instructed then blurted out, "Am

I about to be fired?"

"What?" She laughed. "No. As a matter of fact, I have a proposal for you. The JCC is bringing Bob of Sesame Street here for a fundraiser, and I've been looking all over town for a children's choreographer. Then, yesterday, I'm leaving my office, and I see you teaching right across the hall in the auditorium. I can't believe you've been right here under my nose the entire time! Who knew? So would you be willing to choreograph some numbers for his show?"

She never once said the word "tap," or I would have told her right away I was unschooled in that genre. It wasn't until two weeks later, as she handed me the tapes he'd made of the songs he wanted choreographed, that she said, "There'll be eight numbers for you to do in total: one ballet, four jazz, and three tap. Okay?"

Inside, I gasped with frenzied horror. "MAY DAY! MAY DAY! Ah-OOOO-ga! ABORT MISSION!" To Rose, I smiled warmly and said, "Sure. That will be great."

When I shared the news with my family that night, my husband gasped. "What are you going to do?" he asked. "You've got to tell her."

"I can't tell her," I lamented. "I've already signed the contract, and my name is on all the posters. Plus, a week from today, we're holding auditions." I added, "Honestly, though? I feel like I can do this. I think, if you can dance, you can just dance anything."

With that, I went to the mall and bought tap shoes and, because this was at least a decade before Google, stopped at the library en route back home for a how-to manual. The next seven days found me holed up in our basement, tap shoes on, eyes intently focused on the book in my hands, as I moved liked the snazzy-looking girl in the progression of photographs, commanding myself rhythmically, aloud (albeit at a snail's pace): "Shuf-fle-Ball-CHANGE; Shuf-fle-Ball-CHANGE; Fl-AP-Step, Fl-AP-Step; Step-Ball-HEEL!"

A few months later, when the show was over, and Rose and I were in her office, basking in the joy and success of the production, I finally confessed everything to her. She gaped at me and cried, "You've got to be kidding. I wouldn't have guessed that in a million years." After a beat, she added, "Actually, that just makes the whole thing even better."

Lesson:

*Never allow yourself to fall prey
to self-imposed limits. Geodes, after all,
appear to be just plain brown rocks
until they're tapped open.*

Pre-School Dance Classes

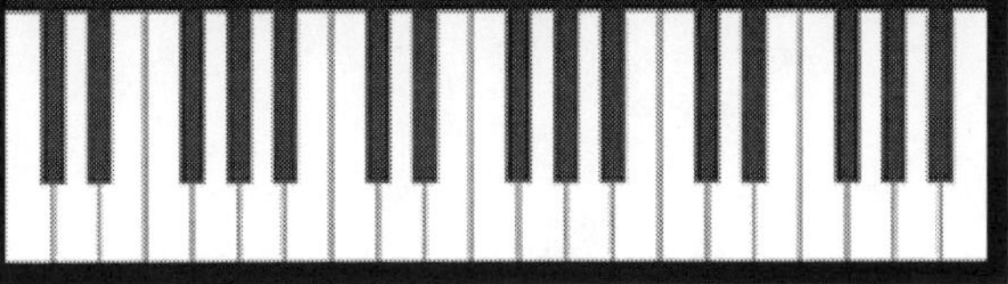

Oh, how I loved my pre-school dancers.
So full of life. So very energetic and
perpetually happy. So very pink and purple.
They lived for their weekly dance class,
and always tried their best.
Plus, they had the most disarming knack
for assessing the people
and situations presented to them
with deadly candor.

7

Appearances

One day, I was feeling glamorous and sophisticated as I swept into the dance studio, wearing my brand new, lipstick-red, hooded, woolen scarf.

"Hey, Shelley," said one of the little cherubs, "why are you wearing that towel on your head?"

A quick glance in the mirrored wall straight ahead, and I realized that, yes indeed, I was not Meryl Streep in *The French Lieutenant's Woman* after all. To my horror, I looked substantially more like Rocky Balboa.

Another time, as everyone dressed at the end of class, one little dancer put her dress on over her leotard, folded her arms across her chest, and said, "There! Now I don't care if the boys lift up my dress; they won't see anything."

"Yeah, why do boys do that anyway?" I asked, seeking enlightenment.

Giving me a look of embarrassed disbelief, she exclaimed, "Because they think girls in short dresses want SEX!" The tone implied that someone my age really should know that by now. (She was four and had three teenage brothers.)

But the best exchange, by far, was during the conversation as we sat in our circle for warm-ups. Age was the topic, and everyone was expected to share. When it got to be my turn, I copped to being five-and-three-quarters, since that made me older than anyone else in the room.

"Really?" asked most of the girls, stunned.

"Yes," I insisted. "I'm just very tall for my age."

I watched as their little wheels turned this information over a bit, comparing and contrasting my maturity level with their own and, possibly, an older sibling's or two. Then I watched, ever so slightly indignant at how quickly that concept was accepted as plausible.

One street-smart girl did finally try to shake some sense into everyone. "You're not five-and-three-quarters!" she shouted out with an edge of disdain in her tone.

"I'm not?" I asked. "How old do you think I am?"

"You're, like, eighty-one!"

"Wow," I said. "Not even eighty."

Lesson:

Always listen when children tell you things.
Even if their conclusions
aren't exactly spot-on accurate,
the undercurrents of their truths
are uncannily close.

8

Stage Fright

Dance classes at the JCC were broken down into ten-week increments. The last week, we would perform all our routines for the parents. We called them "recitals" but, out of deference to the pre-school need for continuity, everything about them was exactly as it had been the preceding nine weeks when no one was watching: floor warm-ups, barre warm-ups, leaps, turns, chassé, a trip to the water fountain, a run-through of each dance we'd learned, a cool-down and, finally, a group bow. And it was held right in our beautiful dance studio, too.

Unfortunately, though, until I acquired some experience, I would be agog when a dancer or two in each class became cowed – sometimes even to the point of tears – by the presence of adoring eyes upon her. It happened every semester. Even in my twelfth year of presenting these shows, I could not predict who would fall prey to it. Fascinatingly, it was rarely the ones who'd been the quiet, reserved, under-the-radar type all semester.

In my third year, one ballerina's experience was so excruciating that it evoked a change in how I dealt with the affliction forevermore.

Her name was Chloe. She was three and as cute as life gets, with huge brown eyes and an equally huge smile. Her vivacity and social skills were off-the-charts fabulous, and she always learned the dances quickly. Never would I have expected this little firecracker to experience angst when the room filled with parents. She just always seemed so confident.

Yet, when I started the music and sat facing the class to begin warm-ups, I panned the line of girls before me and noticed Chloe was glassy-eyed and trembling. I'd learned that sometimes not acknowledging the symptoms, simply continuing on as if everything were just fine, worked to coax a cutie back to participating. But it was always a toss-up what the outcome would be. I spent the first five minutes of most recitals holding my breath and beseeching God for mercy.

I always instructed my little dancers to perform directly in front of where their families were seated "so they can get lots of really good pictures of you." This one time, though, I was so very sorry I had.

I heard my stage-frightened girl's mother start to hiss commands at her in rapid-fire, staccato blasts: "CHLOE! PAY ATTENTION! STOP JUST SITTING THERE! DO WHAT THE OTHER GIRLS ARE DOING! I MEAN IT! DO YOUR WARM-UPS! HURRY UP! GET GOING! I'M NOT KIDDING!"

Surely it wouldn't take Benjamin Spock to realize the folly of this tactic. It's not as if humiliation is ever a motivating force, after all, and, against mounting fear, it borders on just plain foolishness.

As the rest of the class headed to the barre, Chloe remained glued to her spot on the floor, now crying with abandon. I went closer, smiled at her with love, and held out my hand to coax her (hopefully) back into the fold. But she had fallen over the edge.

With immense pomp and drama, her mother stood up, actually pointed at Chloe, and shouted,

"EITHER YOU GET OVER THERE TO THAT BARRE RIGHT NOW WITH THOSE OTHER GIRLS, OR I SWEAR TO YOU, I AM LEAVING! I HAVE A LOT OF WORK THAT I SHOULD BE DOING BACK AT THE OFFICE, AND I AM NOT ABOUT TO STAY HERE AND

WATCH YOU JUST SIT!"

The scene had now reached bona fide debacle status.

My pink-tutu'd little sweetie slumped over now and absolutely howled.

"OKAY THEN!" trumpeted her mother. "YOU HAVE MADE YOUR CHOICE! I. AM. LEAVING."

With that, she actually trounced out of the room.

Chloe bolted after her, screaming as loudly as her little voice could muster. "NO, MOMMY! NO, MOMMY! NO, MOMMY! PLEASE DON'T LEAVE ME!"

A collectively stunned silence shrouded all the adults in the room, as I felt tiny pinpricks along the entire circumference of my eyelids. I offered a rueful, omniscient glance to my fellow survivors, and turned to my remaining dancers.

"Okay," I said brightly. "First position, please. Nice straight dancer backs. Ready? Demi-plié. One, two ..."

When the recital was over, I grabbed some construction paper and markers from the Early Childhood storage room, and drew a picture of a ballerina and her teacher doing high leaps. All around the border, I drew red and purple flowers.

Then I wrote:

Dear Chloe,

Roses are red,
Violets are blue;
You're a great dancer,
And I love you.

XOXOXO
Shelley

I dropped it off in her JCC daycare room. The teacher, after I recounted the horror story, assured me she'd give it to Chloe the minute she awoke from her nap.

From that day on, I always included the following paragraphs in my letters home to parents about the upcoming recital day:

There's a fascinating commodity that performers in the creative arts can fall prey to: stage fright. What's amazing about it is that, contrary to what anyone would think, it can actually affect even the most confident and outgoing of souls. Stranger still is the way it can also be so inconsistent. One time, it may be of no concern at all to a dancer, and, at the next performance, it can make him or her completely freeze up.

I always appreciate how supportive and

enthusiastic the JCC parents are about these recitals. I cannot get over how, every ten weeks, at 1:00, 2:00, or 3:00 in the afternoon, we are dancing to a full house. And, likewise, I understand how disappointing it can be to leave work and then have your cutie not want to dance.

But we're making memories here. So if your dancer simply cannot perform this time, then please give him or her a warm hug, bring that sweetie onto your lap, and enjoy watching the show together. It's still a fun time you're sharing, after all, and you know very well that the minute you get home, that same child will perform every last routine for you with gusto and panache.

Thankfully never again did stage fright ruin anyone's JCC dance recital experience.

Lesson:

Sometimes, the best you can do
is damage control.

Performing Arts Camp

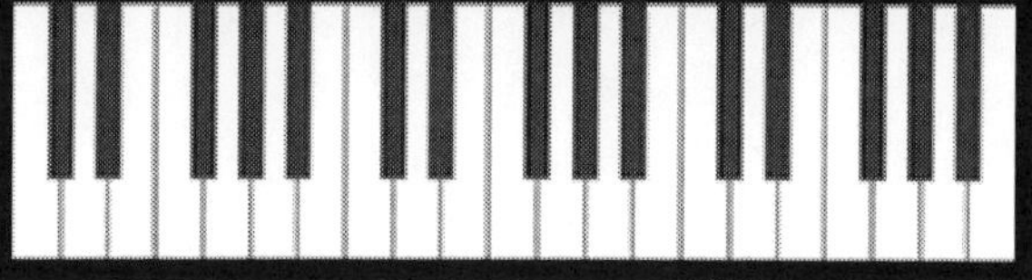

In 1992, a summer performing arts camp
was a groundbreaking idea.
So, of course, my friend and role model,
dynamo Rose Melnik, would be the one to
conceive and institute one at the JCC.
I felt flattered and excited when
she asked if I'd work with her again
and, to this day, I cherish
the precious experiences
from those five years.

9

Far Too Many Legs In The Dance Studio

In the middle of morning dance class with the nine-year-olds, I suddenly noticed someone had positioned a big, fat rubber spider right in the middle of the floor. I gave the class a look of amused omniscience, and they all smiled back mischievously as I headed over to pick it up before we began our floor work.

I decided to embellish on the fun they'd already provided for us by doing chainé turns over to our interloper. Arriving at my destination, I extended one leg behind me and, like a seesaw, elevated it higher and higher as I lowered my torso and arms closer to the prop. My audience was doubled over with amusement. At the last moment, for added drama, I leaped away, then, *en pointe*, returned to it and give it the most delicate of touches with my slippered foot.

It exploded into hundreds of thousands of teeny baby spiders that shot out in every direction, like fireworks, as they tried to find their now-deflated mommy, who was scurrying to a safe hiding spot somewhere beneath the nearest baseboard.

A moment of incredulity descended like a cloak of deathly silence, and then pandemonium erupted. It was the strangest vision of teeny spiders and young, screaming campers both doing pretty much the same choreography of frenzied spirals and spastic turns.

I dashed from the room to get a jumble of wet paper towels from a nearby bathroom, and perform an act of arachnicide. But unfortunately, in my fervor to regain order and control, I neglected to mention this mission to my seventeen-year-old assistant. She imagined she was suddenly a solo act at the worst possible moment in history.

Oh, how relief sprang forth from every one of her facial features as I returned with the munitions, handed her half and, together, we sopped up the pinprick-sized invaders.

All twenty of us spent the remainder of our class time in the lobby, each taking turns recounting our own personal rendition of our collective nightmare. Meanwhile, the custodial staff mopped down the entire dance studio, sprayed it with insecticide, and then mopped it a second and then a third time.

Lesson:

The most creative choreography
one ever creates can be inspired
by the rawest of animal instincts.

10

Keeping Abreast of Current Events

During the same summer as our camp spider adventure, our city government humiliated itself by caving to ten women who insisted that men and women are so completely equal that the law should mandate that everyone who so chose could walk around shirtless. The spokesmodels doing this lobbying became known as The Top-Free Ten.

Our midday routine at camp was to take our bag lunches to the area known as the picnic pavilion, and relax for forty-five minutes. It was located behind the building, and backed up to the bike and jogging path that ran the length of the canal gracing our region.

As I sat with Rose and two other faculty members one particularly warm day, the drama teacher looked down the path, squinted, and said, "Whoa! That almost looks like... oh, my lord, it IS! There's a woman jogging this way with no top on."

One of the campers had spied her, too. In record time, all seventy-six of them, ages eight to eighteen, including the assistants and assistants-in-training, were lined up with their tippy toes grazing the blacktop, fingers pointing flagrantly, as they laughed the raucous, unbridled belly laughs for which children are famous.

"Should I make them stop?" gasped Rose.

"Absolutely not," said I. "Why should she get to be the only one who can make a statement?"

With that, the woman jogged by, her lily-white Coke bottles step-ball-changing with each loping stride.

Lunch ended really early that day. No one seemed to have much of an appetite.

Lesson:

You can learn every bit as much
from a bad example
as you can a good one.

11

The Show Must Go On

Tech Week, the five days before a show opens, is always nerve-wracking. Stress, worry, and fears about what could happen when the curtain goes up are so pervasive, they're practically palpable.

One year, these feelings were made even worse at our performing arts camp by the fact that the campers had been slacking the entire summer. Even by the final dress rehearsal, they still didn't know their lines or their entrances. We, the faculty, were at our wits' end. At least the drama director never lost his sense of humor about it, though, bless his heart.

At lunch, after the morning's frightfully bad full-dress run-through, the music director and I sat there, looking haunted and lobotomized. The drama director chided, "It's easier for you two. You're still young yet. You can leave town, change your names."

We returned to the salt mine at 1:00, and tried one final time to salvage the show.

Rose wrote the plays for camp each year, and this one was particularly clever: What life would have been like if all the Biblical characters had carried cell phones. Very creative and entertaining.

There was a loft perched above the set. where the camper who was playing "God," in a white robe, sat with his back to the audience for the entire performance. When we realized how many lines the campers were forgetting, it struck us what an especially perfect set-up this was. We simply gave God a script to hide on his lap and increased his role to "God and Prompter." His only disadvantage was that, since he couldn't see the stage, he had no idea who was or wasn't present and accounted for.

The best moments occurred in the scene where Biblical character Sarah, age eighty-plus, was supposed to call her husband, Jacob, age ninety-plus, with the news that she was pregnant. Unfortunately, too many campers were milling about in the wings on stage left, and made it impossible for Sarah and her walker to get through in time for her entrance. Jacob had dawdled on stage right for her as long as he possibly could, then finally accepted that he had no choice but to do the scene alone. He was going to have to ad lib.

Looking at his cell phone, then at the audience, he exclaimed, "Oh, look! A text message from Sarah. It says we're going to have a BABY!"

The music started up for this love duet and dance and, thinking quickly, our creative thespian sang adoringly to his walker instead. He then waltzed around the stage with it in a loving embrace. It was too bad, actually, that Rose, in the interest of finding out what had happened to Sarah, had left her seat between the drama director and me, because we were convinced she would have loved this hysterical variation of her play.

With just a one-second blackout – no curtain – the scene was then supposed to switch to ten years later. Sarah was supposed to be in her kitchen, on the phone with God, lamenting about what a handful Isaac had become. Isaac, in turn, was supposed to buzz around her and act as annoying as possible.

The problem, once again, was that Sarah was still nowhere to be found. Worse, the camper playing Isaac was ten in real life too, and only doing this gig because his family had missed the enrollment deadline for soccer camp, and his mother said he had to do something all day. Our camp had openings, so that had been that. He begrudgingly marked time with us each day, and rarely got where he was supposed to be at the right moment.

God deduced something was amiss, having just sat through Jacob's love duet solo, and concluded – rightfully so – that it must now be his turn to ad lib.

"I think I'll call Sarah," he said, completely off script now. He sat there hoping, hoping the musical director would follow his lead and play the ringtone on the keyboard. He did. He stopped after three rings, and God continued. "Hi, Sarah. God here. I know you're not home right now, but I wanted to leave you a message." Jacob and his walker, also completely off-script, hustled onto the stage now to catch the phone.

"God? God? It's Jacob. Sarah's out at the moment. I need to talk to you about Isaac."

Suddenly, from stage right, Isaac appeared, looking totally baffled. He knew this all seemed vaguely like the scene he was used to acting out every day, and yet, at the same time, it was also terribly different. He decided he'd carry on until someone yelled at him and/or explained what he was really supposed to be doing.

He zoomed his little balsa wood plane around Jacob's face, as he'd been accustomed to doing around Sarah's. Jacob had never been on stage for this scene before, and had no idea what the dialogue was supposed to be. Enter God and Prompter.

"I bet you want to shout Isaac's name," he told Jacob.

"Isaac!" shouted Jacob.

"I bet you want to tell him to stop bugging you," said God and Prompter.

"Stop bugging me, Isaac," echoed Jacob.

"I bet you want to –"

"I'll handle this, God," said Jacob, astute enough to realize the scene was looking less amusing and more irretrievably stupid by the minute. "Isaac, I'm on the phone with God. Please go to your room." He pointed the way, and Isaac, totally weirded out by it all anyway, was more than happy to oblige. But with a priceless final flourish of obliviousness, he exited in the opposite direction of Isaac's extended arm.

After the curtain call, the campers gathered in the theater seats for one last critique. Opening night was now just three hours away. Rose, who always lavished grandmotherly warmth and praise and kindness on all her beloved campers, was livid. With her face red and eyes bulging, she read them the riot act for a good fifteen minutes. Ditto for the music director, drama director, and me. The children sat there motionless and ashen.

Then, somewhere in the next hours, a miracle occurred.

The production was absolutely flawless, from beginning to end! No missed cues, no dropped lines, no obstructed entrances.

Absolutely unbelievable and, to this day, we four faculty members shake our heads and shiver at its memory.

Lesson:

Even in retrospect,
there is no comfort or enjoyment
in a near-miss.

12

Finale, Act One

A look at my history and it couldn't be all that surprising that my segue from teaching nursery school and dance to teaching piano, flute and voice came about completely by chance.

One of my original nursery school moms later enrolled her children in the summer performing arts program, and once, near the end of the camp day, she saw me working with one of her daughters on a vocal solo for the show.

"Shelley! You sing and play piano?" she asked, flabbergasted.

"Yes, that's actually what I majored in in college." I smiled. "I just did dance for fun."

"Do you give lessons?" she asked, her voice full of hope.

"Well, I don't, but I certainly could."

"This is absolutely incredible," she said. "Just this very morning, three of my neighbors and I were sitting at my kitchen table and saying how great it would be if we could find a really NICE piano teacher – one who loved kids, and is fun, and not so strict that they hated lessons, but still one who could make them good at music. One of us even said, 'Hey, as long as we're fantasizing here, wouldn't it also be great if she came to each of our houses, instead of us having to go to hers?'"

She looked me square in the eyes. "If you ever decide to change careers, Shelley, you'd have our ten kids as your students right off the bat."

I humored her with a smile and a pleasant laugh, and said, "Alright, thanks." I went on my way, but before even reaching the parking lot, I knew what had just happened. Opportunity was knocking.

The semester before summer camp had begun, I'd sensed a change in the way the powers at the JCC dealt with teachers. They squelched our creativity more and more, and constantly "advised" us on how to run our classrooms more efficiently. At first, I told myself to stop being so spoiled, that no one's job is perfect. I needed to buck up and deal with the changes. The positives still outweighed the negatives by far.

But then, as the semester progressed,

the higher-ups began wanting to change me. I should be less effusive and more understated when dealing with parents, they felt. They strongly suggested I teach more technique and, maybe, fewer actual dance routines in my classes. (To the preschoolers? Good grief!) And, finally, they wanted me to increase the size of my classes to accommodate more members. I disagreed. Nine three-year-olds at a time was perfect, I told them. And ditto for twelve four- and five-year-olds per class.

Fortunately, because I was teaching fifteen pre-school dance classes per week, and a like number of school-age dance classes per week, I had the fiscal clout to stand my ground. But I knew I'd put myself in their cross-hairs by not capitulating, and that, before long, it was going to be a problem.

I had two choices: I could start another school year teaching dance at the JCC, chafing under the scrutiny of non-teachers who knew nothing about the way to run a joyous, successful class. Or I could take a leap of faith in myself and teach the way I knew to be best.

Before camp began the next morning, I sought out the mom I'd spoken with the previous afternoon and said, "I'd love to teach voice and piano lessons to your girls, and to your neighbors' children as well. And I'll do it in each of your homes."

She was so elated she squealed, then jumped up and down, then hugged me.

Even with such hoopla and positive reinforcement, the realization was bittersweet. It was time to trade in my dance shoes for a keyboard again, and return to my roots.

Rose, always in my corner, let me send a flier home with our eighty campers. Three weeks later, when the new school year began, I had fifteen students. By January, it had mushroomed to twenty-five and, by the following September, the roster had swelled to forty.

Lesson:

There is no end
to the vehicles available to transport us
to new adventures.
Test-driving as many as possible
keeps life fun and challenging.

Act Two

Voice,

Flute

and

Piano

Lessons

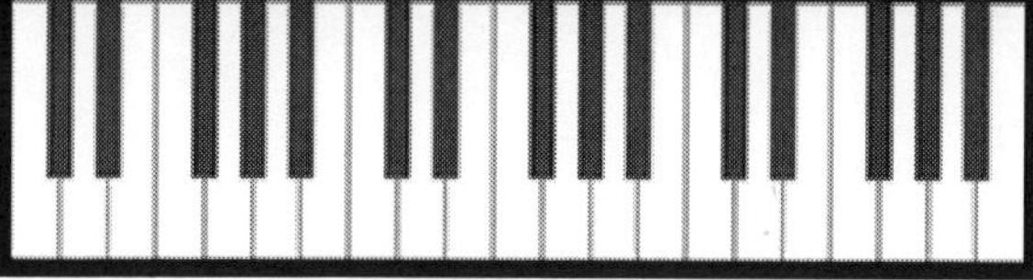

Pets

Teaching is still teaching,
and making learning fun was still slated
as Job One. Some days, though,
that was a lot easier than others.

Not unlike the talk shows
that invite animals and their trainers
to visit their sets,
some of my most memorable times
featured unusual encounters
with pets, too.

13

Having A Ball

In my first year of teaching, I was especially gracious. Never did I voice even the most heartfelt distaste for my surroundings. I was, after all, trying to build a clientele. So, when my assigned seat at a new student's house was between the gorgeous antique upright and Tiki-the-Gerbil's cage, I smiled warmly and simply said, "Thank you!"

With the concentration of a chess master in the final round of play, I locked my eyes on the music, my student, and the majestic piano, and then retreated to that special place in my mind where no rodent could get me.

As Tiki loudly rooted around in her wood chips, I exclaimed to my student, "Oooh! Wonderful phrasing there! And what perfect fingering you used!" And, as fur flew hither and yon from little Tiki as she frolicked on her exercise wheel, I smiled encouragement, saying, "Yes! You made that one sound like a real song. Great work!" But soon, Tiki stood on her legs, holding onto the rungs of the cage like a convict at mail call. With her tiny white claws bulging beneath their flesh, she began squealing rhythmically as my student played *Ode to Joy*. Finally, I could take no more.

"Oh dear," said I, with a smile that belied the revulsion turning to magma-like bile in my throat, "Tiki's making it a little hard for me to concentrate here. Is there someplace else she can go until your lesson's over?"

"Oh, sure," said my helpful little musician. At once, she popped her into a translucent yellow ball that was then set upon the floor.

Ah, the joy Tiki experienced for the remainder of the lesson time as she, encapsulated in her little yellow bubble, did doughnuts all around my dancing feet.

Lesson:

There are times when fifteen minutes is an absolute eternity.

14

Lookit The Birdie

Creatures with long, hairless tails make me scream. Literally. Ditto for the ones with feathers who are granted flight privileges in their homes. They, in fact, make me run and duck and flail my arms a lot. I discovered this one night when Claude, my student's African gray parrot, waddled into the room where I was teaching.

Claude was an avian with a Rhodes Scholar vocabulary and an array of circus tricks that included saying "Meow" when the family cat walked by, and "Woof, Woof" when it saw the two dogs. And, I was told, his greeting every morning, to whomever walked by his cage first, was, "Claude. Want. OUT!"

He challenged me with a mighty glare as he strutted past me, and I began to hear my breathing accelerate. When he stopped dead in his tracks to give me a side-eye, I felt all sensations of warmth immediately leave my fingers. So, when he fluttered to the couch, just inches from my shoulder, I knew I had to change this balance of power at once.

I summoned every ounce of false bravado I had and drew myself up to an imperious, standing position. I pointed at him solemnly and commanded, in my best No-nonsense Teacher Voice, "STAY!" Incensed by such unmitigated audacity, Claude aimed his ample beak at once toward my gaping eyeballs, and turned himself into a feathered missile.

Had my student not been doubled over with laughter, I am sure she would have been much more help. But instead, the cacophony of my screams and frantic footfalls, as Claude chased me around the perimeter of the room, flapping his wings and shrieking his hoarse war cries, caused the matriarch of the house to sense trouble. She dashed in and summoned the crazed bird to her shoulder, pirate style, with a shrill whistle from her pursed lips.

Lesson:

Being bossy isn't always an effective way to deal with subordinates, especially those outside one's immediate jurisdiction..

15

Unexpected Artistry

While her kindergarten-aged daughter, Kate, and their bulldog, Spike, played in the fenced-in yard, one of my piano moms began a beautiful rendition of *Für Elise*, phrasing well, fingering to perfection, and controlling the tempo and expression with panache and aplomb. Just as she reached the final page, though, Kate dashed in, breathless, eyes agape.

"Mom! You've gotta come see this," she shouted. "Spike just pooped an 'R'!"

My student, startled from her reverie, gave a quick glance toward her daughter. Then, as the child's words soaked in, she looked at me with both embarrassment and apology in her eyes.

"Can I come, too?" I asked Kate.

Sure!" she exclaimed. We all hurried to the backyard where, sure enough, there was a plump, picture-perfect, calligraphy-style

"R" in doggy doo.

"Wow, that's amazing," I admitted.

"It really is," agreed the piano mom.

"Do you think Spike is like the spider in Charlotte's Web? Do you think he's leaving us a secret message?" Kate asked with breathless hope and wonderment.

"Maybe," her mother said, straight-faced, not willing to quash this magic moment.

I leaned near my student's ear and whispered, "Yeah, he's spelling out **R**idiculous Family Here."

She smirked and gave me a friendly elbow to the ribs.

Lesson:

Artistry and talent can be found
in unexpected places.
Personal enrichment hinges
on our willingness to explore
every opportunity that is presented
with an open mind.

16

Butterball Gottlieb

It's true that I've had some trying times with the pets of my beloved students but, overall, I've been lucky with them. Most have welcomed me into their homes with enthusiasm and immediate acceptance – even cats, those highly discerning creatures – and I appreciate it. However, a dog named Butterball Gottlieb snarled and bared his little cockapoo teeth at me when I arrived each and every week.

"It's because you wear hats," his family advised. But nothing changed the one time I remembered to leave mine in the car. There was no way around it: the dog simply hated my guts.

Ditto for the youngest of my four students there, none of whom ever practiced. At the onset of our lesson, I said, "So, shall we begin?" She rejoined, "I don't really care." She tossed me a challenging look, right in the eye. The Pippy Longstocking braids definitely belied the demon within this one.

"Why not?" I asked, still in Perky Piano Teacher mode.

"Because I didn't practice at all this week." The antagonistic delight in her tone reminded me of gremlins in a sci-fi film.

Now, with my No-nonsense Teacher Voice, I intoned, "Really? Then whatever will we do for the next half hour, I wonder?"

"I don't know." She shrugged. "I really don't care. I hate piano lessons."

"Really?" I met her defiant gaze with a steely one of my own.

She added, "And I also hate you." The wickedest of smiles blossomed on her face.

With that, I rose and went into the kitchen, where Spawn of Satan's mother was busily emptying the dishwasher, and said, "Um, this piano lesson thing just doesn't seem to be working so well." I went on to share that not only had no one practiced the entire week, but that Child Number Four had also voiced flagrant distaste for me, personally.

Chagrined, the mother paid me, and I returned to the living room to collect my belongings one last time. But, by now, Evil Girl was holding Butterball and, having heard my exchange with her mom, was in full in-for-a-penny-in-for-a-pound mode.

She tossed her feral little furball at me and shouted, "SIC HER, BUTTERBALL!"

Sweeter words had never made their way to little Butterball's ears in his entire life. All his doggie dreams had come true, and he wasted no time following his mistress's command to the letter.

Lesson:

Under the right circumstances, anyone can set world land records for speed.

Kindergarteners and Fashion

Five-year-olds have a unique sense of couture, and are most generous about sharing it.

17

No White Shoes After Labor Day; No Black Hats in October

One day in mid-October, I left the house wearing my favorite hat, a dramatic, broad-brimmed black number that always made me feel *très chic* and very glamorous, to deliver some music to a friend of one of my piano families.

The five-year-old of the house answered the door. She immediately gaped at me, but then smiled and exclaimed, "Hey! I'm going to be a witch for Halloween too! You look just like a witch!" She was very impressed.

Her mother arrived at the door just then, an understated, salt-of-the-earth kind of woman who, I sensed, went out of her way to avoid impropriety every moment of her existence. Immediately horrified by what she'd just heard, she leaped in to try to repair the damage.

"Er...um...uh...I think she means she likes

your HAT!" she offered, probably praying that the ground would swallow her up at once.

Her daughter scowled at her. "Noooo. I mean she looks like a witch." She peered at me with squinted eyes. "See how she has that wild, messy hair and that long, pointy nose? And she IS wearing a BLACK HAT!"

Because I was sure the mom was about to vomit, I broke in. "But I'm a nice witch. I like children; I don't eat them or anything. And look out there." I pointed to the driveway. "That's my car. I don't even ride a broom."

She stood on tippy-toes to follow my extended arm and said, "Oh!" in a satisfied tone. She scampered away, unceremoniously, leaving her traumatized mother to clean up after her.

But the poor woman had no words. Rather, she let her quivering lip and ashen pallor speak for her as her eyes beseeched me with horror and stress.

"I'm a teacher," I explained, with a reassuring smile, "so I haven't had an ego in a very long time. What just happened here I find genuinely hilarious, and it will be one of my most cherished stories forever."

As a matter of fact, it's become my enduring Halloween treat.

Lesson:

Honesty without malice
is one of the greatest treasures
anyone can bestow.

18

Captain of the Fashion Police

"What's your favorite holiday?" I asked five-year-old Kelly at her lesson one day.

"Christmas and Halloween."

"Oh yes, Halloween is one of my favorite holidays, too."

"Well, of course YOU like Halloween," she scoffed. "That's because you're always wearing COSTUMES."

I felt quite taken aback. "I am?"

"Well, yeah." Her tone vibed a silent "duuuh!" She went on, "You've got those leopard costumes – you've got a lot of those – and then you've got those plastic ones."

"Plastic?" I echoed, starting to shrink down a bit in my chair now.

"Yeah, you know – that black plastic mini-skirt and jacket, and then that red plastic miniskirt and jacket?"

"Leather?" I offered this in a borderline whimper.

"WHATever." She rolled her eyes. "And what about all those hats you wear? Those are costumes."

"Um, yeah, I get it, Kelly." I opened her folder, trying to regain some dignity.

"And then there's those millions of pairs of different high heels you have." The girl was unstoppable.

"OKAYYYYY!" I honked. "Let's get down to work here already."

Lessons:

(A)

Honesty without malice
may have to be in limited doses
to be quite as cherished a commodity.

(B)

If you ever need a reality check
about your appearance,
ask a five-year-old.

The Saturday Morning Curse

For the longest time, the earliest lesson on my Saturday morning roster seemed jinxed.

Perhaps it was just too early an hour on the first full day of a weekend for anyone to be expected to be good at anything, least of all piano lessons.

Or, maybe, my own alacrity for teaching waned a bit as I thought about how the rest of my family got to sleep in while I trudged off to work.

I can't be sure. All I can say is that, for a number of years, my hair always seemed grayer by the time I returned home late each Saturday afternoon.

19

Sammy

Sammy was a red-haired, very freckled eight-year-old with an unusually subdued manner, that belied the tempest below. Not only did he rarely talk, he also made absolutely no eye contact whatsoever. I grew quite adept at engaging him in "conversation" by presenting everything to him in "Twenty Questions" format, because he would always either shake his head or nod.

If his mother, a private school teacher, had even the remotest inkling about what I was sure was his autism, she certainly never shared it with me, or acknowledged it in any way in front of him. Every Saturday, I felt as if I were Alice, their house was Wonderland, and I'd fallen down the rabbit hole again.

Sammy did seem to like music, but the progress was glacial. Still, progress is progress, and we managed to make our way by doggedly putting one finger in front of another, week after week. But then came that awful day when his mother asked about the end-of-year recital.

"Well, I do have one," I said, fearing the worst now that I knew her better. (She had been denied lessons herself as a child, and absolutely reveled in Sammy's.) "But I never make the students perform if they don't really want to."

"Oh, Sammy REALLY wants to!" she gushed.

My heart sank. "Hmmm." I chose my next words with the utmost of care, hoping against hope to reach her. "I'm so surprised about that, actually, because my take on Sammy has always been that music is a very intense but personal joy for him. I've always gotten the feeling that he loves it because it's all his own, and he doesn't have to share it with anyone."

"Sammy?" She laughed. "Oh, NOOO! Why, he plays CONSTANTLY for all of us all the time! He LOVES playing for LOTS of people!" (Someone had obviously been pilfering from the stash of Wonderland mushrooms.) She went on, "He's VERY excited for the recital."

I felt nauseated for the remainder of the day, as I envisioned how this was going to play out in a few months for this tortured, sweet child.

Recital day arrived and, with it, Sammy, the epicenter of a self-induced three-foot force field of horror and sullenness so acute it was practically palpable. In front of him, his father and grandfather were snapping photos and cajoling, "Atta boy!" and "Here's the little virtuoso, coming for his very first spotlight performance." Behind him came his mother, flushed with glory and equally oblivious to the agony of her progeny, who was trudging, head bowed, just three steps in front of her.

Sammy dutifully sat in his assigned chair. He even came up to the piano when I announced his name and song. But, when I took my seat in the chair next to the piano bench where he perched, his kept his hands at his sides and his head bowed. I waited a few beats for him to acclimate to his new surroundings.

"Okay, ready?" I whispered finally, for his ears only, in my Perky Piano Teacher voice.

Nothing.

I waited another beat, feeling the audience's fidgety discomfort, which I'm sure he also felt.

"Here's your first note," I whispered to him, my heart aching, as I silently touched Middle C.

And then the tears came in soundless

torrents.

I stood and addressed the audience with my brightest The Show Must Go On voice. "We've changed our minds," I announced with a steady smile.

While Sammy tore across the room to bury his face in his mother's lap, she looked straight ahead, eyes expressionless, mouth stretched wide with a smile fit for a toothpaste ad. I blinked back my fury and gave a warm nod to my next student to join me at the piano.

Lesson:

You should not attempt to construct Norman Rockwell fantasies at the expense of other people in your life.

20

Sammy, Part Two

The following September, when lessons resumed, I arrived on Sammy's doorstep bright and early again. Like always, his bathrobe-clad Ward Cleaver father greeted me and escorted me to the piano. En route to the kitchen, he gave a sing-song call up the stairs to let Sammy know that it was time for his piano lesson.

This time, though, I heard Sammy's door open, and then a pause. I knew at once what was happening: reconnaissance. Sammy was Rambo, surveying his perimeter. Next came the sound of lightning-fast feet on hardwoods, the slam of a distant door, and a flurried, triumphant lock.

Ward stopped dead in his tracks, did an abrupt about-face, and attempted father-like authority as he intoned, "Samuel Robert, you unlock that bathroom door this minute and come down here for your piano lesson."

By now, June Cleaver, in fluffy blue gingham robe and matching jammies, had joined him at the banister.

Sammy projected, as loudly as his lungs allowed. "I AM NOT COMING DOWN, AND YOUUUUUUUU CANNNNNNNNNNNNNN'T MAAAAAAAAAAAAAKE MEEEEE!"

June whirled toward me and gushed, "He really loves piano lessons."

"I'm thinking he really doesn't," I told her, having had enough of her unabashed absurdity.

"Samuel, I'm going to count to three," Ward said, giving another lame go as Serious Dad. "One...two..."

Nothing.

"I'll go talk to him," June said. "Why don't you go take a lesson with Shelley." (Translation: "We have to pay her anyway, so we're damn well going to get something out of it.")

"Splendid idea!" he said, and stepped forward six inches to cross into the living room, where I'd had my ringside view of everything that had just transpired.

"Good morning, Shelley," he boomed, as if I'd just arrived. "Sammy is a little under the weather today, so I'm going to take his piano lesson. How about if I take out my guitar and we jam?"

Ward Cleaver. Jam. Somehow, I'd managed to get a heaping helping of June's Wonderland mushrooms myself.

"Oh, that would be great," I said, and somehow, miraculously, managed to sound genuine.

From the piano bench, Ward pulled out a Wynton Marsalis book, still in as pristine a condition as the day he'd bought it (this, no doubt, because he'd never once opened it), and began to strum some chords in a key nowhere even close to the music before us.

Strum, strum.

"Um, Shelley?" said Ward. "Where are we?"

"We're on measure two," I said in Perky Piano Teacher mode.

"Oh, yes."

Strum, strum.

"Um, Shelley? Where are we?"

"Middle of measure three," I answered.

"Oh, yes."

Strum, strum.

"Um, Shelley?"

Twenty-six minutes to go.

Sighhhhhhhhhhhhhhhhhh.

Lesson:

No job on earth
is worth the price of your sanity.

21

Lloyd

At his initial lesson, Lloyd spent the first ten minutes in the next room with his mother, defiantly insisting that he would not sit at the piano until he had finished his breakfast. His mother tried valiantly to assure him that the bagel would stay fresh for thirty minutes. She even told him that, if he would just "be a good boy and take a lesson," he could have two bagels when he was done.

Judging by his round cheeks and bulging tummy, she'd made these kinds of deals with him often in his mere eight years on the planet. Nonetheless, this time, probably because she was mortified by how obvious it was to me already that theirs was not a picture-perfect household, she relented and let him come in for his lesson clutching the butter-soaked bagel in his plump little hand.

"Now Lloyd," she chided, "when Shelley

says it's time to play, you're going to have to put the bagel down."

Yeah, like that was going to happen.

At our next lesson, Lloyd came into the room in full Confederate soldier attire – brandishing a sword, no less. "Isn't he a STITCH?" his mother laughed. "He just cracks us up constantly."

Oddly, I wasn't nearly as amused. Perhaps I'd lost my sense of humor when he informed me, the minute his mother had left the room, that soldiers don't have to play songs they don't like or take orders from girls.

"They do if they want candy at the end of their piano lesson," I informed the little renegade. Mission accomplished.

Another time, he came in with a beret tilted crisply to the left, and two curlicues drawn in black pen from just below his nostrils to the middle of his fleshy cheeks. He spoke with a French accent for thirty minutes. "Oh, Lloyd, you are such a RIOT!" his mother chuckled on her way out of the room.

"I weel nut be playing zee songs in zees books," the artiste informed me. "Zay are stuPEED and ugLEE." I refrained from voicing the first response that came to mind: "You mean like your ridiculous fake mustache?"

I opted, instead, for, "A true Frenchman can turn them all into musical masterpieces."

The most grueling lesson, by far, was when he'd started off grumpy and belligerent anyway and, when I'd said it was time to sightread a two-line song, he actually threw himself onto the floor and flailed his arms and legs. Never having experienced anything like it before, he was completely astonished when I squawked at once, with vehemence, "Are you KIDDING ME?" I sprang from my chair, stood over him, scowling and pointing, and commanded, "You come sit on this bench at ONCE!" I locked my eyes on his until he was re-seated. "Exactly what seems to be your problem?" I asked, casting Teaching Etiquette to the curb.

"I DON'T WANT TO SIGHT READ," he bellowed insolently, his teeth clenched for effect, arms folded tightly across himself.

"Well, let's compromise then." I knew full well what he wanted was not to work at all. "How about if you just sightread one line, since that's really all the time we have, now that you've wasted so much of it kicking and screaming on the floor."

"I....................D O N' T...................
COMPROMISE!" he shouted, getting nose-to-nose with me.

"Then you are going to have a very hard

life." I slit my eyes.

Karate-chopping one different note on the keyboard with each syllable, he spat out, "I. AM. VERY. MAD. AT. YOU!"

"Know what?" I now took a torch to any and all Teacher Etiquette I'd ever learned. "I really don't care." He gaped at me, and I added, "This lesson's over. You're dismissed."

He stomped out of the room and was replaced by his gentle sweet-dispositioned older brother, who gave me a smile of commiseration. Just then, Lloyd stomped back into the room and actually had the chutzpah to challenge me. "Hey! You forgot to give me my CANDY!"

I said, flatly, "Boys who throw tantrums don't get candy."

He ran back into the kitchen and threw himself to the ground yet again, kicking and flailing. Now, though, he was on his mother's time. Permanently.

Lesson:

To "discipline" does not mean to "punish,"
it means to "teach."
It is the responsibility of all adults
to discipline the children in their lives.
Shirking that responsibility jeopardizes
everyone's well-being.

22

Joey

This sweet boy is still in my prayers to this day, twenty-five years later. "Please take care of him," I whisper. "Please let him be okay."

Joey was a fourth-grader when I met him, living in a house where it seemed as if someone had shoveled a six-inch-wide path for me from the front door to the piano ten feet away. The Irish Setter had a half-dozen spots of mange on her back the size of silver dollars and for the first five months of Saturdays, I watched the same blob of grape jelly on a nearby end table morph from an oval of sticky goo into an ever-burgeoning culture of foamy white mold. Eventually, it became powdery and wafted, with the help of the heating vent below, onto the carpet.

Joey himself, though, was irresistible. His luminous brown eyes just melted me. He was eager to learn piano, and had an undeniable ear for music. But patience was definitely not his strong suit. All too soon, the novelty of lessons wore off, and he forgot about practicing until late on Friday nights, right before bedtime.

He had so much creativity in him, though. Every week, I would marvel at his latest displays of vivid, beautiful watercolor paintings. He had a penchant for landscapes. His creations were exotic places from his imagination: secluded waterfalls with verdant flora that burst forth from the mist below, wooded pathways with variegated carpets of moss and lichen, full of color and form and texture. I never saw such detail and precision from someone so young. It was obvious how loaded he was with talent in the creative arts. That was why I was so convinced I could entice him back to letting music stoke that side of him again.

But then came the morning of the ambush.

The mom, a chronically unsettled, jittery woman, seemed more tightly wound than ever when she greeted me at the door. And my exuberant Joey was unusually quiet and on guard, eyes darting furtively across the floor. Something was very, very wrong here.

Suddenly, from the couch in a dim corner, obscured by the opened door, Joey's father's chilling tone cut through the air. "I'm selling the piano," he said with a punishing antagonism that delighted him. I looked over at him, refusing to seem fazed at all, since watching people flinch was very obviously this man's blood sport.

His wife broke the silence with loud, imploring moans and rasped to me, "He's mad because Joey doesn't practice."

I then watched with incredulity as she actually got down on her knees in front of him, encircled his legs with her arms, and wailed. "Please, Joe. Please don't sell it. Please. Joey will practice. I mean it. I promise. He'll practice."

"He's nothing but a LIAR!" the father exploded. "He says he'll practice, but does he? He certainly does NOT. The kid's just a liar. Aren't you, Joey? You're a liar. You're nothing but a LIAR."

Joey hung his head and cried silently as I stood there, sickened by how ugly this scene was.

"Joe," I began with warmth in my tone that I certainly didn't feel. "This is so typical of piano students everywhere. I kid you not. My own daughter and I go through this, too. Believe me, I know this feeling of frustration. My father even went through it with me. I shirked practicing shamefully often. But it ebbs and flows. There are times when we, as parents, have to nag about practicing, and just as many times when we don't."

"I'm selling the piano," he repeated viciously. "End of discussion."

"Well, that's truly a shame," I said, now with a disdainful bite to my tone, "because your son has talent. You'll be seriously limiting his potential." I turned to Joey, gave him a really good hug, and said, "I'll miss you, Sweetie. I have LOVED having you for my student. I'll think of you every day. You're a wonderful boy. You're special, and you're talented, and you're fabulously creative. These are things no one can ever take away from you."

Before I could even reach the door, the mom ran from the room, crying loudly, leaving her son alone with the sadist he shared a name with. I disdained her even more than the husband. I blew Joey a kiss from the porch and left, still not showing one sign of fear or stress, until I pulled into an office parking lot a block away. I called the next three students on my roster and canceled their lessons, and then I cried for the next hour-and-a-half.

On Monday, I had an emergency meeting with the principal, the psychologist and the guidance counselor at Joey's school, to tell them what had transpired and to elicit their help. I knew they meant it when they assured me of how much they appreciated my input, and that they would do everything they could to ensure Joey's well-being. They also said that, by law, they would never be able to report any outcome back to me.

I always look for Joey whenever I attend shows for local artists. I check the right-hand corner of every watercolor I ever see, landscape or not. Mostly, though, I hope I'll just catch sight of him in the commonest of places – the drug store, a restaurant, the gas pump – and see someone with him who's obviously on his same page, and who adores him, and someone he adores right back.

He'll look happy and at peace, and far beyond the tortures of his childhood.

Lesson:

There will be times when, after you've done
everything that you possibly can,
you are left with no alternative
but to pass the baton
and trust that the next person will have
your same passion and sense of purpose.

Car Srories

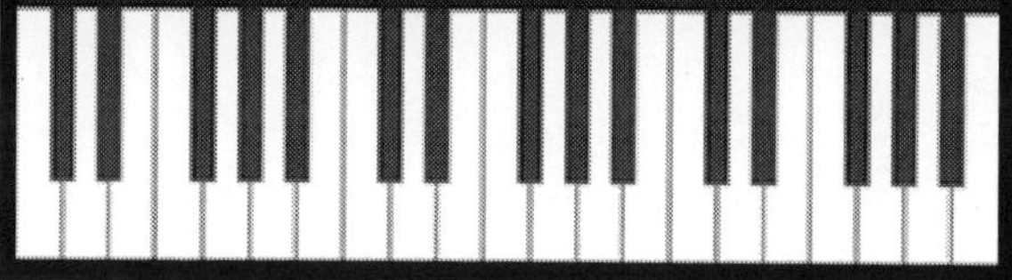

*In any line of work that requires travel,
the means of getting from Point A
to Point B is an integral part of life.*

23

All in a Day's Work

It's been said that clothes make the man and that hair makes the woman. So I'm wondering, maybe a little fearfully, if the contents of a car are what makes an itinerant voice, flute, and piano teacher. If so, I'd be deemed quite suspicious by even the most optimistic of people. One look in my vehicle and you will find:

1. A big handmade tote bag with vivid musical prints, festooned with pockets in many wildcat print designs and colors, each a different size, one full of cash and checks;

2. An enormous plastic container full of every kind of candy imaginable (as students who have excellent lessons get "one piece for each talented hand");

3. Two colorful plastic crates filled with

Dollar Store prizes, bestowed each time a student completes a book or learns how to read music in either clef;

4. A small box containing the tips cut from the fingers of a bulk purchase of latex gloves, used to sheath a student's finger before it is plunged onto a stamp pad, to leave a fingerprint on the front of his or her piano folder (as with the candy, students earn one for each talented hand and, when the folder is so filled up with ink spots that no manilla color is visible anymore, the student receives a Dollar Store prize); and

5. a really expensive flute.

Now picture the driver in a leopard hat, matching high heels, and a black plastic mini skirt and jacket.

Lesson:

Sometimes you have to be a little eccentric with your methods in order to achieve the results you know are best.

24

Forced Retirement

I loved taxiing between lessons in Star, my Jetta Trek. (Get it? *Star Trek*?) I found her perfect for me from the moment I saw her: lipstick red outside, black upholstered inside, with a sunroof I could control with the touch of a button. In fact, just about everything about her was button-activated: the seats, the windows, the locks, the trunk, the hood, the gas door. She made me feel like a traveling musician, hip and savvy.

But, as with other close relationships, the traits that one adores at the beginning can be the same ones that make one crazy by the end. If I'm fair, though, I have to admit that a big part of my disillusionment with Star happened because I didn't let her go when I should have, and she retaliated.

I'd push the remote to activate her locks, and she'd make her trunk pop open. I'd try to open her sunroof, and she'd respond by having the windows in all four doors go down instead. I'd push the button to eject the gas door, and I'd watch the hood pop up. The final straw for us, though, came the day she engaged her alarm system each and every time I turned off her engine. The only way I could vanquish her sirens was by running around, like a Keystone Cop, to the passenger's side and inserting my key into the lock. This, in turn, made all four windows go down... on a day when it was pouring.

She made us a laughingstock, and so I banished her from my life. Still to this day, when I run into families I haven't seen in years, they will laugh and say, "Hey, remember that day when it was raining so hard and you had that red car..."

Lesson:

If you allow things their dignity,
and don't push them beyond their limit, then
you're more likely to avoid
an endless aftermath
of humiliation and pain.

25

Yo Ho Ho

The day I had eye surgery, a mom called to ask if she and her eight-year-old daughter, my piano student, could bring me some cookies they'd made. Touched by their thoughtfulness, I said, "Sure!" But when I caught a glimpse of myself immediately afterward, as I passed a mirror, I worried that the surgical patch on my left eye could be very unnerving to someone so young.

Thinking quickly, I tied a leopard bandanna, buccaneer-style, around the top of my head, clamped on one big gold hoop earring, and secured one of my daughter's big stuffed penguins onto the top of my shoulder. (Just my luck – thirty stuffed penguins in that room, yet not one parrot.)

As soon as I saw the car pull into our driveway, I dashed outside. I even shaped my index finger into a hook for extra effect.

But, wait. Oh gawd; it wasn't them.

My husband exited the passenger side, and we gaped at each other.

"Honey!" he exclaimed, still gaping.

"Bobby!" I gasped, finger still aloft and hook-shaped. "What are you doing here?"

By now, the driver was beside us, the Sales Manager from the car dealership not far away, there to take me for a test drive in this lovely vehicle.

"Argh!" I said to him, figuring, as long as it was this ridiculous, I might as well just go for broke. "Mighty fine vessel ye got here, Matey."

All he could do was stare. (A speechless car salesman? This was epic.)

We went for the drive, and I decided that, yes, I did, indeed, like this vehicle and want to purchase it. We scheduled an appointment for the following afternoon to draw up the necessary paperwork.

The next morning, I had an appointment with the surgeon to remove the patch from my eye. When he finished, he handed me an enormous pair of post-operative sunglasses and instructed that under no circumstances was I to remove them for the next twenty-four hours.

I went to the car dealership at our pre-arranged time. As I entered the Manager's office, I saw the light of understanding jump into his eyes. It read, loud and clear, *"Ohhh! NOW I get her!"*

Dashing over and graciously extending his hand, he asked, "And who are we today – Jackie O?"

Lesson:

Today's humiliations
will be the favorite stories
of one's future grandchildren.

26

Punctuality at All Costs

I was halfway through Saturday lessons, as I basked in the warmth and glorious sunshine of a May day, drinking in the sight of vibrant bursts of red and yellow tulips I passed as I drove between lessons. I savored the smell of the air, redolent with lilacs and new grass, wafting into my open windows. I drank in the beauty of the Spring sky, blue as cornflowers, and filled with cotton-ball clouds. All day long, the students had shown great progress with their recital pieces, and I stoked the fantasy of how perfect that event would be just two Sundays from now. Life, indeed, was good.

Suddenly, I realized that the sirens I'd been hearing for the two minutes since I'd left my last student's house were actually getting closer. Then I saw why. An enormous fire truck sat parked in front of a house one cul-de-sac over, and firefighters and neighbors were swarming the area. I had only moments to act before I would fall prey to the barricade heading my way and be delayed indefinitely. I took a quick left, then an equally quick right, and did, indeed, avoid the barricade. But alas! The fire hose running right down the middle of the street gave me a moment's pause.

Knowing that time was of the essence, if I were going to make it out of this labyrinth of streets – the kind with trendy names like "Trevor Trail" and "Caitlyn Court," after the developer's obviously adorable children – and back onto the main drag, and meet the students left on my day's roster, I was going to have to be a little ingenious. Perhaps even a little like James Bond.

Oddly enough, driving with the fire hose between the left and right sides of my car's undercarriage seemed like the perfect solution. Or at least it did until I hit a metal joint on the fire hose and got stuck... and made the hose stop pumping water onto the smoldering house one block back.

I tried, frantically, to wrest my car's chassis from the hose clamp, listening all the while to the firefighters shout, "WHAT THE HELL HAPPENED?" and "WE GOT NO PRESSURE! SOMEONE GO CHECK ON THIS DAMN HOSE!" and, finally, "HURRY!"

Men in shiny yellow raincoats and helmets dashed into view in my side mirror now, as did lots of curious neighbors. Suddenly, the screams sounded downright mutinous. "ARE YOU FREAKIN' KIDDING ME OR WHAT? THIS BROAD ACTUALLY DROVE RIGHT OVER THE HOSE!"

It took several of the fire fighters to hold down the hose – on their bellies, no less – while I backed up and freed my little car from the impinged joint. The fire chief came over, purple-faced, veins bulging across his neck, forehead, and temples, and screamed, "YOU GET THIS CAR TO THE CURB, LADY, AND DON'T. YOU. MOVE. IT. AGAIN."

The neighbors all glowered, and watched with great anticipation for me to get my due, as the sheriff came to my window to ask for an explanation. "Well," I began lamely, "I teach piano lessons..."

He listened politely, then went back to his squad car with my license, registration and insurance card in hand. I quickly called my husband for back-up. "Bobby, come quick! I'm in really big trouble. I'm somewhere near Lindsay Lane."

Upon the officer's return, he asked where my proper license plates were.

These are the only ones I know about," I said honestly, feeling a black dread starting to creep into my stomach.

"These are improper plates. As of March first, they were no longer supposed to be on your vehicle. Did you receive new plates in the mail, Ma'am?"

I gulped and said, "Yes, in February. But I thought they were for the car I bought my daughter in January."

"And where are they now?" He threw me a stern look, likely trying to decide if anyone could really be this vacant, or if he were on the receiving end of the world's most convoluted snow job.

I sounded like a four-year-old when I replied, "On her car...at college." I added, "Tomorrow is her birthday," and smiled lamely. I have no idea why.

"Well, Ma'am, I can't let you drive this vehicle with improper plates. I'll do you a favor, and I won't impound it. But I'm going to take the plates, and you won't be able to drive it until the proper plates are on it."

"But they're on my daughter's car... at college," I said once again, still in my involuntary baby-talk voice. This time, at least, I had the dignity not to include the nugget about her birthday.

"Yes, Ma'am, I understand that," he said politely. "There's also a potential fine of $75 a day for each day since March first that you've been driving with these improper plates."

"A DAY?" I gasped, doing the calculations in my head with an algorithm that included teaching piano lessons to infinity and the sale of potential grandchildren.

He added, "And the fire chief feels you've damaged the hose, and that will probably cost at least eighteen hundred dollars."

Just then, two firefighters, screwdrivers and my improper plates in hand, smiled nastily at me and symbolically gave me the hardware that had been securing the plates to my vehicle.

"Do you have a ride home, Ma'am?" the officer asked me politely.

"Yes, I've called my husband," I managed to choke out.

"And you'll need to get this vehicle removed from here, too." He smiled, still very patient and polite.

"I have a towing service." My voice now constricted to an out-and-out whisper.

But when I called Triple A, the operator explained, with an impatient little bite to her tone, that, without license plates, my car could not be towed by them.

"But I live just a tiny ways down from here." I watched the fire truck leave, and the neighbors all turn their stares now on me and my outlaw car. Tar and feathers were just moments away; I could feel it.

"I'm sorry, Ma'am," she said, with a strident, punishing edge in her voice. "That is our policy."

My husband appeared just then. Because of the roadblocks, he'd had to hoof it from the main drag down to the inner chambers of the development, but his instinct had told him to follow the sounds of the firemen's walkie-talkies in order to find me.

He was kind enough not to laugh as I expounded on (and on) about how my day had spiraled from "quite ideal" to "a complete nightmare" in just forty minutes' time. He didn't even lecture, either, bless his wonderful heart. He simply drove us home.

Miraculously, there at the kitchen table sat our college girl, who said she couldn't really explain why but, all of a sudden, she'd felt she'd wanted to drive home for her birthday. Best of all, she even had my plates in her trunk – in their original envelope, no less – because she'd realized, from the beginning, that the ones on her car already matched what was on the registration card.

Quickly, we trekked back to the scene of my crime, got my vehicle up to code, and then drove back home to start the birthday party a little early... and with copious amounts of wine.

Lesson:

In the card game of life, sirens, emergency vehicles, and, most of all, fire hoses, trump piano lessons.

Familiarity

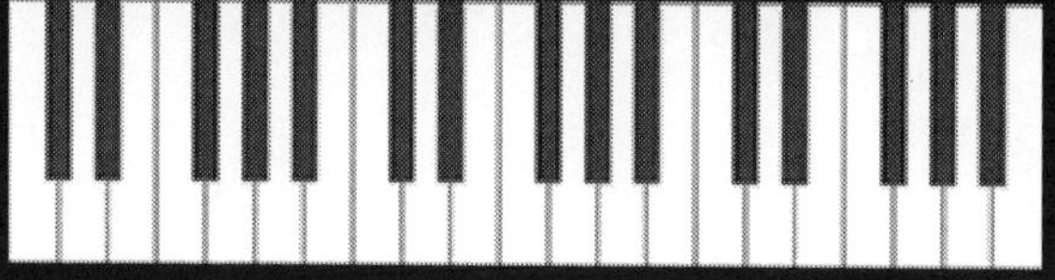

Familiarity

I have been visiting some families' homes for so many years that the guards normally in place when a non-family member is present are not only down, they're downright non-existent.

27

If You Give a Mouse a Cookie

A brother-and-sister team who'd been with me for seven years greeted me at the door one day with the news that their grandma was there for her annual visit. She and I exchanged our pleasantries, as was our custom, and, while I sat down at the piano, she headed off in the direction of the kitchen.

Less than a moment later, only deafness could have prevented me from hearing her caw loudly, "LUCY, THERE ARE MOUSE DROPPINGS BEHIND YOUR COOKIE JAR!"

I didn't know how long this visit had lasted so far, but I knew immediately that Lucy had already had about all she could take of her husband's mother.

Without even realizing how very self-incriminating this response was, she snarled back, with impressive disdain and ferocity, "I KNOOOOOOOOOOOW!"

Lesson:

To an outsider, the line between horror and hilarity in a family can sometimes be a very, very fine one indeed.

28

Conflict Resolution

I was in the snow-caked driveway of another long-time piano family, checking cell phone messages before heading to my next lesson, when I looked up and saw the garage door open and the back-up lights of their oversized sport utility vehicle. Knowing the matriarch of that household to be in Perpetual Overdrive, I pitched my cell phone to the back seat and threw my own car into reverse with Danica Patrick-like speed.

In one fluid motion, I skidded across the untended layers of ice and slush and careened into a snowbank at the driveway's edge. I leaped from my car and yelled the piano mom's name, while flailing my arms in her rearview mirror's line of sight. Sighing with relief, I saw her brake lights flare, at last.

"What the heck did you do?" she shouted, as if I were one of her four kids instead of their teacher. (I'd like it on the record, however, that, inside her house, this same woman is a paragon of social grace. She always serves me a heaping mug of the best coffee of my week, always gives me a choice of flavored creamers, and consistently takes care to do so within minutes of my arrival. Also, if she isn't home to serve me, herself, she has left instructions for one of her middle schoolers to carry out the task.)

This night in her driveway, though, I was a thorn in her side, and all niceties were tossed to the curb. We all have our days, after all, and there was a price to be exacted for my having contributed to hers.

"Well, I saw your back-up lights," I tried to explain, "and worried that you wouldn't think to look because piano lessons were over with. You would have probably figured I was long gone. So I hurried to get out of your way, but then I slid on all this ice and snow in your driveway."

She pushed past me. "Never mind," she said, exasperated. "I'll take care of it. I'm really good at this kind of thing." I pressed my lips together hard so the words, "With a driveway this messy, I bet you've honed it to an art form," wouldn't jump out and accost her.

Instead, with warmth and appreciation

in my tone, I said, "Okay. I'll push."

This made Miss Congeniality stop her locomotive-like trek toward my disabled vehicle, turn, and look at me with unbridled scorn. "This is NOT a job for someone in a short skirt and high-heeled red boots," she scoffed.

Rather than reminding her that high-heeled boots dig into ice and snow better than flat-bottomed ones do, or that fifteen years of teaching dance gave me good, strong leg muscles, I opted to demur to this warrior princess. "Oh, okay, Margie," I said with an amused smirk. "You go ahead and take care of this all by yourself." With a full-out smile, I added, "And thank you!"

She barged her way into my car, revved up the engine and then floored it.

Was I wrong to feel jubilant as I watched it fishtail further and further into the snow-bank, and deeper and deeper into the rut in her driveway? Adding to my delight, she rolled down my window and barked, "Your car sucks!"

Having just spied a big four-by-four manly-man truck heading our way, I shouted to her, "Hey, Margie! I think I just found the perfect job for someone in a short skirt and high-heeled red boots." And with that, I jetted out to the middle of the street, waved my arms, and used my best Damsel in Distress pout when asking the driver if he'd be willing to help me. It must have been even more effective than I'd hoped, because his passenger rushed to my aid as well.

Two minutes later, I gave my heroes – and Margie – a big friendly wave as I headed to my next student's house.

Lesson:

In the same amount of time
it takes to get surly and exasperated,
you can also get resourceful.
But only the latter
helps you solve your problem.

29

Leaf Me to My Playtime

If I'm fair here, I have to admit that familiarity is a two-way street. One Autumn afternoon, I arrived at the house of a piano family who'd been with me the better part of a decade. I couldn't help but marvel at the three enormous heaps of velvety, raked-up leaves in their yard.

I did ignore the first pile en route to the front door. I even fought back the urge to jump into the second. But the third one was the biggest of all, and dangerously close to the path where I walked. I finally gave into the tempting reverie of my childhood days in the country, and jumped onto it, back first.

I was still plucking leaves out of my hair when the mom answered the door. "Oh, Shelley!" she exclaimed, concerned. "Did you fall?"

"Well, sort of," said I, flushing. Just then, my student's little four-year-old brother came rushing to the door.

"Shelley just jumped into our leaves!" he tattled, all breathless and wide-eyed. The mom blinked at me and then suppressed a giggle.

"But isn't she a grown-up?" he asked, thoroughly perplexed.

"Not today," she told him, smiling delightedly at me, shaking her head.

Lesson:

Your loved ones will understand
that sometimes the need for an indulgence
simply cannot be averted.

30

Motherhood

I've bestowed the gift of music on, literally, hundreds of – possibly even close to a thousand – children over the course of the past thirty years as a teacher. My own child, however, was not among them. Her, I ruined.

She was eleven when I knew our last piano lesson together had arrived.

We finished up, and she said to me, quite conversationally, truly with no malice or snarky undertones to the question: "So, do your other students, you know, like you?"

I sighed with the wearied resignation of a race-track fan who sees her horse is so far back there is no hope for a victory. "Okay, you don't have to take piano lessons anymore." I furrowed my brow.

"I don't?" she asked, with almost inaudible incredulity, fearing she was surely going to waken from this euphoric dream at any moment.

"No," I sighed again.

It was then I saw her truest innate talent: recognizing and accepting a great offer the moment one was presented.

"OKAY!" she exclaimed, and ran to her room on cheetah legs... you know, like before I could even so much as consider changing my mind.

Lesson:

We are given offspring in this life
to ensure that we remain humble forever.

31

In Sickness and in Health

I remember my dentist telling me that, during the first year of practice, his exposure to so many germs left him frequently sick but, after that, he never fell ill again. With one exception, that's been the case for me, too.

The virus that got to me had only one symptom – a continuous, searing burning sensation beneath the left side of my face. But it lasted for six weeks. It tormented me, whether I worked or stayed home, so it really made no sense to cancel lessons. Plus, I found that, most days, the students and their music kept my mind occupied enough to mitigate the agony.

Except one fateful evening, at 8:15, when I arrived for back-to-back lessons with a brother and sister who'd practiced exactly zero times since last I'd seen them.

As the lesson wore on, my frustration

level mounted, my patience ebbed and, at 9:20, when their very nice mother conscientiously asked how their lessons had gone, I heard myself respond, with no warmth or whimsy in my voice whatsoever, "They sucked." With that, I'd exited their house.

Before I reached my car, however, common sense – and, yes, horror – finally clicked in. The severity of my faux pas not only dawned on me but reached epic proportion, as I thought of the five other houses of students I had on this street alone. When I arrived home fifteen minutes later, though, I felt it was too late to attempt any damage control. Besides, with my face burning worse than ever, there was no way I would have had the capacity to assuage anything.

At 7:20 a.m. the next day, however, en route to my first lesson, I called their house, babbling on about my facial malady, my reduced patience, my poor judgment, my extreme embarrassment. The mom halted me mid-mea culpa. "Oh no you don't," she said, making my heart lurch into my esophagus.

I waited for words of outrage and indignation, followed by "you're fired." But, to my astonishment, instead I heard her say,

"I told those kids that if SHELLEY says you sucked, you must REALLY suck, because Shelley can always find something nice to say about ANYTHING! We apologize to YOU. This will NEVER happen here again." (And it never did.)

Lesson:

If you make enough hefty deposits,
when you need to make an emergency
withdrawal, you're covered.

Holidays

Holidays

The impact of the holiday season
affects not just families.
Its highs and lows,
rewards and punishments,
carry over to piano teachers
and their students as well.

32

Let It Snow

I live in the northeast, in a spot where the winters are long and fierce and bitter-cold. And, until a simple yet life-altering incident fifteen years ago, I used to despise every interminable minute of them.

The first snowfall of that year began the Monday before Thanksgiving, as I was en route to a 7:00 a.m. lesson. I felt chilled from the inside out, and surly, as I left the warmth of my car, faced the frosty air, and even made shallow imprints with my boots all the way to seven-year-old Danny's back door. But then I rounded the corner of his house, and the holiday spirit overtook me.

He was sitting at his family's picnic table, wearing a vivid blue snowsuit, a bright yellow scarf, and the biggest smile this little face could possibly produce. His nose and cheeks were magenta. With the index fingers of both gloved hands, he pointed at the two-inch tall, one-inch wide snowman he'd somehow managed to pinch together from the light, meager dusting of snow that had accumulated before him. The joy and delight in this little sweetie's face rekindled all my own childhood excitement about winter and the holidays, and put everything into its proper perspective.

To this day, whenever I feel a twinge of exasperation about having to shovel, or feel irritated when the heating bill arrives, I think back to that morning in Danny's backyard, and the snowman we shared. And just like that, all my aggravations turn to folly.

Lesson:

Although you may not have control
over what happens in your life,
the effect it has is always up to you.
You're exactly as happy or as miserable,
at any moment, as you choose to be.

33

The Holiday Greeting Pin

My jewelry of choice, one week in December, was a pin that had been bestowed upon me at the Dollar Store in an act of appreciation by a man I'd let go ahead of me in line. It was a round, white lapel pin that showcased a green "L" surrounded by a red circle, with a diagonal line across it. No "L." Get it? Noel. Very cute.

I wore it to all my students' lessons, challenging, "Can you read my pin? It's a holiday greeting." The kids, regardless of age, saw the "L" for exactly what it was: a letter. Almost without exception, they solved the riddle within moments.

But nothing could have been further from the case with their parents. To them, the "L" had to represent something. Suddenly, my perky little greeting became a sort of Rorschach test.

Two moms, both with workaholic

husbands who I see only on recital day, thought the pin said, "No Love." Similarly, one of the dads, who's a bit of a smarmy ladies'-man type, thought my holiday greeting was, "No lovin'?" (Eww.)

A psychiatrist mom, with a predominantly female clientele, suggested that the pin I was showing to every child I taught read "No Lesbians," while a dad, who's a bona fide candidate for alpha male poster child, boomed with conviction, "NO LOSERS!"

A couple who'd been living for months under the duress of home renovations both said, independently of each other, "No angles?" while "No Life" was the offering I heard from a sleep-deprived mother of four, as she removed socks and underpants from beneath the piano bench.

But the best guess by far came from an elderly woman I teach, who knows I'm Jewish but lets me come into her home every week anyway. She read my pin, blanched, and guessed, "No CHRISTMAS?"

Lesson:

The older you are, the more difficult
it can be to see life
in its purest, most lighthearted form.

34

The Dreydl Song

For the majority of piano teachers, the song they absolutely forbid any of their students to play in their presence is 'Heart and Soul." There are only so many repetitions a person can take in a lifetime.

But I would gladly listen to – and even participate in – a thousand choruses of "Heart and Soul" if I never again had to hear even five notes of the over-sung Hanukkah song "I Have a Little Dreydl." (So WHAT if I'm Jewish?)

With all the gorgeous melodies my tribesmen have composed throughout the centuries, how this obnoxious little ditty ever came to be so universally recognized and sung, I cannot understand. To me, it is the Jewish equivalent of "This is the Song That Never Ends." All I know is that I flatly refuse to allow my students to play it.

This all started my fifth year of teaching,

when I had an exceptionally large Jewish clientele, and a copy of "The Dreydl Song" that I doled out to them all. By the last day before vacation, four weeks later, I had to go to that Safe Place Where No One Can Hurt Me in my mind every time a student began to proudly serenade me with it.

Finally, after finishing the lesson at the very last house on the last day before December break, my adorable little eight-year-old student bestowed a gorgeously wrapped box upon my lap.

"Happy Hanukkah!" she shouted. "Open it now!"

"Okay." I began tearing away the beautiful blue and gold foil paper. Inside was a large, expensive-looking mug in blue and creamy white, with lavish Judaic designs all over it. "Oh, this is spectacular!" I exclaimed.

"Pretend you're drinking out of it," my little angel urged.

"Okay," I smiled, loving her enthusiasm.

I put the cup to my lips, tilted my head back. and heard a tinkly music box play very loudly: "I HAVE A LITTLE DREYDLLLLLLLLLLLLLLLLLLL."

That beautiful cup has a permanent spot at the very, very back of my mug cupboard. And there it will be for generations to come. I know this because I made my husband cement it to the shelf paper.

Lesson:

One must take whatever steps necessary to avoid madness.

35

The Holiday Song Challenge

"Oh, this is one of my favorite Christmas carols," I said to nine-year-old Emily, placing the music in front of her. "Do you know it?"

"'Away in a Manager'?"

That was the day I decided I needed to do my part to ensure that holiday music – banned now from many public school curricula – would not become extinct for the children I love.

"Whoever learns the most holiday music during the month of December wins my piano bag," I declared, in the flier I gave to each student.

My piano bags are one-of-a-kind because I make them myself before the beginning of each new school year. They have lots of pockets on the outside to accommodate pens, my glasses, a small notepad and, of course, the cash and checks I receive along the way. The fabrics that comprise these unique creations are an amalgam of animal prints and musical designs which, I do realize, sounds hideous.

But, honestly, when pieced together, they make for a fabulous finished product. (I know what you're thinking: This from the woman who wears plastic miniskirts and weird hats?)

Anyway, the plan worked. All month long, every time they completed another holiday song, my students were allowed to affix a sticker to a leader board that I schlepped to each lesson. The competitive juices flowed, and the beautiful tunes of the season did as well.

By the end of the first year of the challenge, the winner ended up having to learn fifteen songs, including "Away in a Manger," in order to squeak by everyone else. Later, several of my more advanced students wisely pointed out that their versions of the same holiday songs as the younger kids' took longer to complete, since they had so many more pages, thus making the challenge unfair.

So, I changed the rule to: Whoever learns the most PAGES of holiday music during the month of December wins my piano bag. Last year's winner was a staggering NINETY-TWO PAGES OF MUSIC!

Best of all, the comment I heard most frequently, when lessons resumed in January, was, "Next year, I'M going to learn the most pages of holiday music."

Lesson:

Anyone can improve
his or her corner of the world.

36

Holiday Lifestyles of the Rich and Cheap

I have a group of students who have each amassed a repertoire of at least fifty two-page songs, and they are the ones I send out on gigs when people call me requesting "background music" for their special occasions – cocktail parties, office soirées, even Communion parties and Bar and Bat Mitzvah celebrations. The students enjoy it because they're doing something they love, while getting paid for it. I love it because it's great experience for them, and builds their confidence and musicianship. The clients love it because they get professionally played music at student prices. Everyone's happy.

But there's another reason I started this service, an extremely selfish one: I just hate doing background music gigs myself. They don't challenge me, they don't comfort me, and I sit there wishing I had my little fingers on one of those snazzy and luscious-looking crudités, rather than the thin, polished, unyielding slabs of ebony and ivory.

One Christmas season, a socialite acquaintance of mine told me she needed a pianist from 11:00 a.m. to 1:00 p.m., for a mid-week luncheon she was hosting. This meant that all my little prodigies were going to still be in school, and that I was going to have to do the gig myself.

I arrived, at the designated hour, in a crepe and sequined red Christmas ornament of a dress, replete with matching sequined red stilettos for which Dorothy from Oz would have mud-wrestled me. This was showbiz, Baby! I didn't want it ever said that I wasn't into the spirit of the occasion.

Adrianna, the self-proclaimed "profess-ional party planner," highly bronzed, per-fectly coifed and expertly lip-lined, met me at the door and deigned to accept my mere cloth coat and remand it to the utility closet in the kitchen. She assessed my ensemble, dismissed me in her mind as a carnival person, and then led me, officiously, to the reconditioned antique Steinway grand next to the glittering ten-foot-tall Christmas tree.

She stayed while I set out my binder of music, twisted the knobs on the sides of the bench, and adjusted the music holder to eye level. Then she waited an additional few minutes while I played, satisfied that, since my hands were now busy, they'd probably no longer be able to pocket any of the expensive-looking knickknacks all over the room.

The air swaddled me in the most comforting, delicious combination of roast duck, garlic, bubbling spiced fruit, and Bayberry candles that I'd ever known. It wafted in and out of my nostrils from the kitchen, as I played Silent Night. It swept by me with each passing guest, as I Fa-la-la-la-la'ed my way into rounding out a perfect Norman Rockwell experience.

As I neared the end of my music binder, I surreptitiously glanced at my watch and noted that I had only fifteen minutes left to play. The problem was that the luncheon, for all intents and purposes, was really just starting to hit its stride. I knew that, if I just abruptly closed up the piano at 1:00, pulled my coat out from next to the broom and left, the ambiance of this picture-perfect moment in time would be absolutely ruined.

I had ninety minutes still left before afternoon lessons would begin, so I made the executive decision to flip my binder back to page one and play on.

The champagne punch kicked in around

1:00, and several of the socialites on the couch next to the piano tossed off their Manolos and launched into enthusiastic tell-all's about their BFF's in other rooms of the house. Doyennes in designer ensembles and serious jewelry would trickle in and out and, the moment they were gone, I would get an earful of how much it was rumored they just paid for their latest vacation home, diamond necklace or liposuction.

Just for fun, as I turned a page with one hand, I played as softly as I could with the other while the most vociferous of the heiresses was at her catty, caustic best, scandalizing her hostess's inferior choice of caviar serving spoons. Her derisions rang out like Santa's finest sleigh bells. I fervently hoped that my boss had been within earshot.

Bad, Piano Gig Girl! Bad, bad, bad! Where's your Christmas Spirit?

Finally, at 2:25, there were just a few stragglers left, so I unceremoniously found my coat, still in Cinderella's closet. I bid goodbye to Adrianna who, I'm imagining, must've had a helping (or several) of the champagne punch by then, because she behaved quite warmly and effusively to me now. So ebullient was she, at this point, that in fact, I half-expected her to invite me along that afternoon to her next tanning session.

That night, after lessons, I stopped back at the house to pick up my check. Because the hostess was related to one of my piano families, and someone I had a fairly comfortable acquaintance with myself, I'd gladly – yet, I feel, still rather generously – given her the "student rate" for the gig. She had it ready for me in cash when I arrived, but it was the amount for only two hours' time.

I smiled warmly at her, and said, "I worked until 2:30, though. Did you realize I did that?"

Her eyes became glaciers. "Oh?"

"It's just that, at 1:00, when I was supposed to go, the party was in full bloom, and doing so beautifully that I didn't want anything to ruin it. I genuinely felt that my getting up right then and leaving you with no more live music would've been a horrible faux pas."

"I see," she said, and made herself push out a purse-lipped smile. It was actually way more like an annoyed grimace. I knew, without question, that had we not had her relative as our mutual acquaintance, this discussion definitely would not have been anywhere even close to over.

Instead, she turned abruptly, yanked her Fendi handbag from the antique coat rack with inlaid gold filigree and a ball-and-claw base, pulled out a Williams-Sonoma calculator, and figured my bilking fee out to the last begrudging nickel. Included in the ransom she was being forced to hand over to me were four one-dollar bills, three quarters, two dimes and five pennies.

I heard my snow pants jingling, ring-ting-tingling, with each frosty stride to the door.

Lesson:

Even with pounds of tinsel and gold foil
to draw attention elsewhere
and obscure the view,
a Scrooge will never go undetected.

The Many Faces of Musicianship

Music's effect on people
is as individualized
as the personalities and lives
it touches.

37

Giftedness

I have a provocative poster that a psychiatrist friend of mine got from a pharmaceutical rep. The entirety of the middle third is a headshot of Beethoven. It merges vivid whorls of color and musical notes across his face and hair, and then changes abruptly to black and white as it stretches and distorts his features, enlarging them, and roiling the whorls out of proportion the rest of the way across the page.

Calligraphied across the top of the poster is an encouraging sentence about how manic depression enabled Beethoven to create works of vast diversity and depth. It is so superior in its advertising prowess that it leaves the reader thinking Ohh! I wish I had manic depression. Beneath Beethoven's dramatic rendering is the name of a prescription drug company, a little blurb about timed releases and easier peaks, and a calendar its patients can use to check off their daily dosage.

I put a crimson matte around the top and bottom of the poster, leaving only the design of Beethoven for display. It hangs in a thick, gold frame on the entry wall of the music room in our house, right next to my piano, and makes a dramatic and dazzling focal point that I enjoy every day while I practice. To me, it represents a perfect depiction of the turmoil that raged within all three of the gifted students who've graced my life.

The one common denominator I recognized among these talented and somewhat tortured souls was their unspoken fear that their gift was in charge of them, not vice versa. They never did, after all, ask for it in the first place. It seemed to pigeonhole them far too early in their lives, and left them feeling as if they had no say in their desire to explore other options. The well-meaning adults in their families would extol how lucky they were to have something so special given to them, but I always watched the impact of those words overwhelm and defeat them. What if they couldn't measure up? What if they didn't want to become a piano virtuoso? Would their relatives still like them?

They were on the receiving end countless times, even in my presence, of such familial goadings as, "I can't believe you're doing such an easy version of that piece. I know you could play something a lot harder than this."

Despite my assurances to the parents and grandparents that learning piano is a process, and my promises that everything would come in good time, they pushed their little prodigies shamelessly.

In all three cases, these children responded in the only way they thought they could: with passive aggression. They practiced as little as possible, gave next to nothing at lessons, and advanced at a snail's pace that belied their tremendous potential. My heart ached for them. It truly did. But with only thirty minutes to spend with each student per week, I had no chance to undo a week's worth of parental pressure.

I sadly watched as my three little Beethovens turned their backs on their gift, because it wasn't allowed to flourish and develop naturally and over time. What started out for them as beautiful whorls of color and vivid possibilities, once discovered by others, abruptly turned to unrelenting tempests of black and gray that extinguished all desire.

Lesson:

An artistic gift is not only a rare treasure, it
is an extremely delicate one
that, when misdirected,
may be sacrificed forever.

38

Talent

Talent is innate ability fueled by personal discipline, drive, and showmanship. It is different from giftedness in that, first, it's far more common, and, second, it draws others to you rather than sets you apart from them. Plus, it doesn't limit or define who you are as much as it gives yet another facet to your personality. The one down side I've seen of talent, though, is that, if overexposed, it can lead to the loss of humility.

Nothing, but nothing, rankles me more than a self-impressed, cocky student far too big for his or her britches. But I've found that the fastest way to cure young musicians of such tendencies is to place a piece of music before them one or two levels beyond their ability, and ask them to sightread it. In less than ten minutes' time, they and their talent get a much-needed reality check.

Lesson:

Remaining humble when you have talent is the highest form of talent there is.

39

Solace and Consideration

The students who've plucked at my heartstrings the most, over the course of my career, are the ones who turn to the piano in times of stress, to calm themselves down and overcome the pressures of their everyday lives. There are not many of these students, but I recognize them at once.

More times than not, they're the quiet, overachiever kind of spirits, always eager to please. Some I've even heard from, via their parents, after they've gone on to colleges for degrees in subjects totally unrelated to music. "Johnny was all wound up about a physics test he'd been studying for," they'll tell me, "so he actually went into one of the practice rooms in the music department and played some of his old songs from when he took piano lessons with you."

At the risk of offering a really bad pun here, I must admit that those kinds of messages are music to my ears. They not only give me a burst of pride and pleasure at what music has come to mean to my students, but also resound within me on a personal level.

My daughter loves to share the story of how, when she was sixteen and learning to drive, she could always tell how well or how poorly she'd done behind the wheel of my car by how long I had to sit and play the piano when we returned home. "And if I ever heard Tchaikovsky," she'd add, "I knew I'd done an especially bad job."

Lesson:

Music has innate, restorative powers so tremendous that they border on magical. It is not a coincidence that it has been a part of every culture, on every continent, since Time began.

40

Desire and Determination

When an instrument other than voice is involved, progress can still be made even when innate talent isn't abundant, but desire and determination are. I see this most often in my adult students, who've waited decades to learn to play. They work doggedly because the desire to fulfill their dream spurs them on, and brings them great feelings of accomplishment between their intermittent bouts of frustration and impatience.

So far from over-confident and self-possessed is this group that they mitigate every compliment or word of encouragement I ever bestow. I'll say, "That was very nicely done. Your counting was accurate as can be, and you played every single note correctly and with confidence."

They'll cast their eyes downward and reply, "Well, I don't know if that's the case."

"No, it IS!" I'll insist. "I'm very happy

with the job you just did."

They'll say, "Yeah, but this music is written for six-year-olds."

"It's written for students who are beginning the piano," This correction comes with a smile.

"Well, probably I could have done it much better," they'll say.

At this point, I would arch my eyebrows and use a playfully stern tone. "Okay, from now on, when I give you a compliment about your musicianship, I want you to say, 'Thank you, Shelley.' Do you understand?"

They'll look at me sheepishly and nod, visibly amused.

I'll continue, "Let's practice. You did a wonderful job on that piece. I'm very proud of you."

They'll smirk and dutifully respond, "Thank you, Shelley."

Unbelievable as it may sound, I actually have to repeat this drill with them often. They'll play their assigned piece for me, I'll comment on it favorably, they'll respond self-deprecatingly, and I'll say crisply, "I'm sorry. Did I just give you a compliment on your musicianship?"

Guilt-ridden, they'll bow their head and say, "Thank you, Shelley."

But they're diligent workers, every one,

and a great source of pride and satisfaction for me as I watch them improve each week.

Wait. Was that another compliment? Well, come on then, grown-ups! What do you say?

Lesson:

If you take it to heart when people
criticize you, constructively or not,
then it is only fair
that you acknowledge compliments
for what you've done that was excellent.

41

Illusions

Siobhan was an extremely talented soprano with gorgeous red hair and an equally radiant voice. She was the first student I ever took to Solofest Competition, a forum where budding musicians play and/or sing graded pieces before an adjudicator, and receive a score from him or her, as well as comments about the performance.

My talented girl definitely knew her piece, a level six, the highest degree of difficulty, and remembered each and every nuance we'd worked on to perfect it. I was her accompanist for the performance before the adjudicator. By the end of the first exceptional measure, goose bumps covered my body.

After her performance, I left, as protocol required, while Siobhan did the sight-singing portion of the competition. I waited for her in the hallway, full of pride and delight.

When she emerged from the room, not five minutes later, her face was the exact same color as her hair, and she was sob-crying.

"What is it?" I gasped. "What's wrong?"

"I did HORRIBLE! He went on and on about all these things I'd done wrong on the piece, and I totally messed up the sight-singing. I was terrible at everything."

I stood there, dumbfounded, and re-ran the entire performance in my mind. What had I missed? I wondered when I had become complacent and lackadaisical with this girl, hearing only what I wanted to hear, rather than what was actually being sung. How long had I been so oblivious? Why was I not more on top of this?

I suggested we go across the street for some lunch until the results were posted. A half-hour later, I trudged back to the school, dreading having to read the completed assessment awaiting me. Siobhan waited at the restaurant, trembling, defeated, and totally unhinged. As I read her sheet and the adjudicator's comments, I felt punched in the stomach for the second time in less than an hour.

"Siobhan, what a lovely, well-trained, beautifully-placed young voice you have! And how well you mastered this very difficult piece! Watch your cut-offs on measures 6 and

27; you held these notes one beat too long each. Your diction is wonderful overall, but avoid making your "oh" sounds so dark that they become like "ooh." Your sight-singing went well; you missed only one note!"

Grade: 6A+ (97/100)

Lesson:

Successfully encouraging a teenage girl
is one of the greatest challenges
of any adult's life.

42

The Exception

Before Cassie, I'd always insisted: "Everyone is teachable."

Nope. Wrong. Very, very wrong.

Cassie was nineteen, model-beautiful, and staying for the summer with her college roommate's family, my neighbors. The roommate herself had been my dance assistant one summer at the JCC performing arts camp and, after that, had taken voice lessons from me. Cassie, like my former dance assistant, was majoring in musical theater.

She was peppy, charming, and an exceptional dancer. On her urging, I attended a gig she was doing as a magician's assistant at our local theme park, and found her to be engaging and full of pizzazz and charisma on stage. The rest of the audience loved her, too. Far more than the magician, it was Cassie who effortlessly stole the show.

She wanted to sing, with all her heart, and worked fiercely toward that goal. But it was about as absurd an endeavor as Jimmy Fallon trying to become America's Next Top Model. My daughter, ten at the time, summed it up quite well after being home during Cassie's initial lesson at our house: "Whoa! She sucked!"

For the first time ever, I did not know what to do, educationally speaking. The girl could not hear where the notes were and, even after struggling to get her somewhere in their vicinity (think Montana to New York as opposed to Croatia to New York), the tone could only be described as caterwauling. My Little Voice reminded me: "Only twenty-five minutes and three more months of lessons to go."

Desperate, I called a music professor friend of mine with twenty years' more experience. "Try getting her to match the pitch of your actual voice, rather than just the notes on the piano," he advised.

"I've tried that," I said.

Silence.

"Good luck," he said, not even trying to suppress his laughter.

I was in a quandary. She worked so diligently, always had the words memorized to the songs I'd assigned, always performed with heart and gusto. But she was just comically bad. In fact, I truly had to hold my breath a great many times just to avoid breaking forth with peals of laughter.

By the end of the third week, taking her hard-earned magician's assistant money was consuming me with guilt. But the alternative, saying, "Cassie, I can't give you voice lessons anymore because, although you're beautiful, vivid on stage, and an extremely talented dancer, your singing voice takes me closer and closer each week to an aneurysm," didn't seem right either. And, since we were neighbors, it wasn't as if I could fabricate a tale about being called out of town unexpectedly for the rest of the summer.

Had I been one of her mentors in the musical theater program at school, or someone with whom she intended to study for longer than a summer, somehow I would have found the words to discourage her from pursuing voice training. But that was obviously not the case here.

So, I did the only thing I could under the circumstances: I told her about the fabulous course my colleague was teaching, that offered summer voice lessons for college credit.

"I'll miss you," I said, "but this way, you'll

get a jump on your credit hours for the fall."

To this day, my professor friend refuses to take my phone calls.

Lesson:

Knowing when to be forthright
and when to pass the buck
is a crucial life skill.

43

The Edict

My basic philosophy of music lessons has always been that, if it's not fun, we have completely missed the point. But it has to be fun for me, too. And, if students don't practice, thirty minutes can seem interminable. That's why I developed "The Edict," a law I lay down to little slackers that goes as follows:

"This was a really bad lesson today. And, last week, your lesson wasn't so great, either. I have a rule about lessons, and it's this: you can't have more than two bad lessons in a row, or we are done playing music together forever." (This usually evokes big, saucer-sized eyeballs.)

"Your parents are paying a lot of money for these lessons. When you don't practice, I feel as if I'm stealing money right out of their purse or wallet," (more big eyes) "and no way will I be going around feeling like a thief. So, if you want us to keep doing lessons together, then we can't have even one more bad lesson. Do you understand what I'm saying to you?" (Still with bug eyes, they nod.)

I then repeat this spiel in the presence of the parents, so that we're all on the same page.

One of two things then happens: either I get a call mid-week that says, "Suzy has decided she doesn't want to take piano lessons anymore," which is fine with me, since poor Suzy was obviously not enjoying herself, OR I never have another problem with Suzy again for the remainder of her time with me.

Lesson:

You do children no favors
if you don't insist they do their best.

44

The Invention

In our school district, the fifth graders are required to invent something that makes their lives easier. One student of mine, who'd begun doing multiple-page pieces, came to her piano lesson actually wearing her creation.

It was constructed from the detachable "skeleton" inside a construction worker's hat – a wide, white plastic band that encircles the head, attached to a matching band that runs from forehead to nape and intersects with a third band that runs from ear to ear. To this infrastructure, my student had hot-glued the stick of a rubber-tipped drum mallet, and positioned it on the portion of the plastic band midway between her eyebrows. Holding the completed creation in place was a dark brown chin strap.

She had the look of a unicorn recuperating from brain surgery.

"So, what have we here?" I asked, entering her living room.

"It's the invention I made for school. You know how I always have to stop when I'm playing my pieces now, and lose my hand position because I need to turn the page?"

I nodded.

"Well, this is my Automatic Page Turner."

"Oh, now this is pure genius," I said. "Please give me a demonstration."

"I haven't actually tried it yet to see if it works," she admitted. "I wanted to save this part for when you came."

"You are always so thoughtful," I said, smiling.

She opened her music, played to the bottom of the page, and gave a quick, excited smile my way. Leaning forward toward the book, she touched the mallet's rubber head to the page and executed a vigorous swipe. The entire tome went careering into the air and onto some knickknacks several feet away, scattering them in every direction.

Hearing the commotion, her mom hustled in. "What happened?" she gasped, then saw her horned inventor and understood at once. "Oh my," she said, as her daughter's eyes welled up.

"Hey, did you know that Thomas Edison had something like 500 botched attempts before he ever succeeded with an invention?"

As I presented this bald-faced lie to the child then before me, I gave Back-Me-Up-Here eyes to her mom.

"Oh yeah; that's true. I remember that," the mom colluded.

"Really?" our little unicorn asked.

"I don't remember the exact number," I said, back-pedaling, "but it was a lot."

"A real lot," my co-conspirator affirmed.

The inventor waited a beat, then shouted, "Hey! What if I clamp the book onto the piano before I start? That way, it can't move."

"Oh, there you go," the mom said, encouragement ringing through the room. We watched with satisfaction as enthusiasm and hope returned to our little girl's eyes.

(Neither of us mentioned that, if the book were clamped to the piano, the mallet wouldn't be able, then, to move the pages that needed turning. Why mess with the success we were having just smiling and nodding?)

Lesson:

Sometimes, it is necessary to use
unorthodox methods when lending support
and reassurance to someone
who's trying something new.
After all, it's not easy for a person
to stick out her neck
and still keep her head together.

45

Rewards

I discovered that one of my music professors was an anti-Semite the day, long before "political correctness," when he was lecturing about a composer who'd performed before kings and queens throughout Europe, and was so exceptional that he even dazzled the Pope.

"This pontiff," the professor expounded, "was so impressed that he allowed the musician to kneel down before him and kiss his Ring!"

I asked a Protestant friend of mine a few seats over, "Wait. That's an honor?"

"Are you kidding me?" shouted the professor, whose musician's ears had overheard my question. "Of COURSE that's an honor. It's one of the highest honors imaginable! Certainly the Pope would never allow some non-believing JEW to kiss his Ring!" He choked as if he were about to expectorate.

This was a private college where class sizes were extremely small, and everyone on campus knew each other. I was sitting in the next-to-last row and, as the room hushed and the professor's scathing bigotry hung in the air like a guillotine, all my fellow music majors turned to see what my reaction would be. Thinking quickly, I, too, turned to glance behind, since it was obvious at once that the man in charge of my grades had no idea I did not share his religious tenets. But alas! Staring back at me, in the last row of our class, was Kawaazi Getabutu, the foreign exchange student from Africa.

Slowly, I turned back around to receive not only my classmates' stares but, now, our professor's as well. I saw the little imaginary light bulb above his head illuminate and make a connection, as he looked hard at me – my thick cascade of unruly auburn curls, my prominent nose, full lips. I watched him hasten to his attendance roster and scan down the names until he found mine, and I watched the wattage switch up a notch.

I never again got an "A" in that class. Despite the fact that my roommate and I studied together and, so, had similar answers on essays, hers would came back decorated with "Wonderful point!" "Excellent choice of comparison!" and "Nicely done!" scrawled across the top.

Mine, on the other hand, would be on the red ink receiving end of "Vague!" and "Exactly what point are you trying to make here?"

I had to accept that I was in a bit of a bind. I wanted to protest such obvious unfairness very, very much. But this professor was the only one who taught this course, and I needed it in order to complete my degree. Certainly, I didn't love getting a substandard grade but, by the same token, I surmised that it would reflect far worse upon him than upon me, since I had high marks everywhere else on my transcripts.

Today, when I sit in on high school, middle school and, even, elementary school shows or concerts where my students are performing, when I'm at a lesson with a student who is doing particularly wonderful work, or as I'm mentoring a high schooler of mine who's become so proficient at piano she can now take on students of her own, I have one thought that can immediately cover my entire body with goose bumps – even the scalp beneath my cascade of unruly auburn curls: It was worth all the hassles and aggravations you ever caused me, Dr. Gestapo, because what I'm feeling right now trumps anything lousy you ever did.

This child, at this moment, has made it all worthwhile.

Lesson:

Always ask yourself:
Will more be gained in this situation
by speaking up, or remaining silent
and biding my time?
Then act accordingly.

Nursing Homes

My students and I do
one nursing home gig per month,
and now that we know
which ones to patronize,
they've become a source
of unabashed pleasure and delight
for everyone involved.

46

History and Evolution

My students like nursing home gigs because they provide an opportunity to perform without the anxiety borne of the year-end recital, where parents and other relatives are present, and expectations are high. At nursing homes, the students get to play before the world's best audience – people who are older, appreciative and, more times than not, hard-of-hearing or asleep.

The residents like our performances because they provide a welcome infusion of music and children, two of their all-time favorite commodities, into the humdrum of their everyday lives. Plus, for forty-five minutes straight, no staff members annoy them.

I like these gigs because they give me a chance to assuage the guilt of a debacle from my youth, and repay a debt which I doubt I will ever feel I've satisfied, Jewish Guilt being what it is.

At thirteen, I went to perform in a nursing home, along with a dozen other voice students from my teacher's studio. It was my first time ever in such a facility. As I sat there waiting for my turn, looking out at the residents, all in various states of infirmity, it dawned on me that, at one time, these people had been my age. They'd even been my parents' age once, as well, with vivid lives and, probably, really good stories to share. Yet, now, here they all were, sad, decrepit and discolored.

A lump the size of Jupiter began to fossilize between the golden vocal chords that my beloved teacher praised each week. When it finally came my time at the microphone, all I could do was stand rigidly, fingers clasped at my waist in perfect "Performance Position," as I'd been taught, and try to swallow. The accompanist played my intro and then, with perfect professional panache, waited a beat after I missed my entrance before returning to the beginning to give me another crack at it. My eyes and the burgeoning orb in my throat began to grow, and I could feel prickles stinging me all over my head.

Intro number two came and went, and my fingers, still in Performance Position, became frozen in an alabaster death grip. I stared, unblinkingly, at the sea of wheelchairs and wizened skin.

Finally, mercifully, when intro number three brought not one sound from between my clenched teeth, one of the high schoolers, cued by my voice teacher, came over to me, put an arm around my shoulders, and walked me kindly off stage. A raven-haired college girl in a blue, spangly costume and fake eyelashes began belting out a song. I hightailed it out to the lobby, pale and shaking.

En route to the car, my father, simultaneously my biggest fan and harshest critic, told me he was ashamed of me. He told me that those people were looking forward to something good, and I had a talent I could have offered. If I'd put the focus on making them happy, rather than how badly I felt, I could have enriched their lives.

So, I owe these people some good times.

Lesson:

Good deeds are much easier
and more satisfying to complete than chores,
even if the job at hand is exactly the same.

47

Nursing Home No. 1: Too Harsh

I have learned, the hard way, that each nursing home has a distinct and definite personality, and that performances by the same students can be received very differently in each place. When I first began doing the nursing home circuit, I elected, naively, to go to one I'd experienced as an audience member when my daughter had been thirteen. Her traveling summer camp had visited there one Friday afternoon, as part of their weekly community service agenda.

The camp's director had said, "If you sing, I want you to get up there and sing. If you dance, go on stage and dance. If you play an instrument, bring it with you and play a song."

One boy, however, had obviously foregone any type of musical education. But, since all campers were required to participate, his contribution to the program came in the form of a rather insipid poem he'd written entitled something like, "My Puppy."

It was definitely not a good poem. The meter was off, the words didn't rhyme very well, and the text didn't even exactly make sense. But he was thirteen, after all, and doing his civic duty, so a pass was certainly in order. But, then, the recitation began to run a little long. Finally, an exasperated resident, smack in the middle of the audience, reached the end of his patience. He shot up from his chair with youthful exuberance and, with a big, dismissive wave of his arm, shouted, "AWW, SHUDDUP!"

So, not knowing any better, imagining all nursing homes were this way, this was the audience I selected for my own beloved students to entertain on our maiden voyage. Miraculously, they all seem to still love me anyway.

It was a Sunday afternoon performance, and the room was both enormous and filled to capacity. This was an EVENT. Many of the women even looked as if they'd dressed up for the occasion. But beware! Experience had already proven that these were no awe-struck patrons of the arts. These people were the *NY Times* critics.

I led off the program by singing a number

from *The Music Man*, and then introduced my stellar performer, Jessica, a polished sixteen-year-old voice student, who did a beautiful rendition of "Summertime" from *Porgy and Bess*. As she took her bow, a cantankerous woman in the front row groused loudly to her companion in the next seat, "This is IT? I thought we were getting a PROFESSIONAL group. Oy, let's hope this doesn't last very long!"

The next sling came from a man in the second row, when I introduced, "Arabesque," by Friedrich Burgmueller.

"WHO?" he shouted out.

"Friedrich Burgmueller," I repeated with a nice, warm smile in his direction.

"Never heard of him." He gave an irascible jeer. "Can't they play something good, like Frank Sinatra, for God's sake?"

"Hmmm. How about if I have that on our program for next time?" I offered, my Little Voice inside my head ominously warning "May Day!"

"And Perry Como, too?"

The mutiny had begun.

"Yeah, and more Tommy Dorsey," shouted a woman who I thought had been asleep.

"And Bing Crosby," trumpeted still another.

"Wow, it sounds like we're going to have to come back here several times." I had reverted to my pre-school teaching days, when we'd gotten off-track during story time.

"And bring PROFESSIONALS with you next time too, will ya?" crabbed the woman in the front row.

Lesson:

You can please some of the people
some of the time and some of the people
all of the time,
but sometimes you can't please
even one soul.

48

Nursing Home No. 2: Too Quiet

The pervading feeling at the next nursing home I chose for us was "Very Proper." The room, large and tasteful, was set up with the meticulousness of a military event. The residents filed in quietly, and without needing to be scolded even once by any of the personnel on hand. There would definitely be no outbursts from this crowd. In fact, the only conversation I remember overhearing was between two women, sitting near the front, and it was exchanged before the program got underway.

A piano mom with a professional camera and a penchant for preserving memories of special events snapped two photographs. "What was that?" the first woman asked in a whisper.

"I think it was lightning," her friend answered back, equally hushed.

The room was windowless.

Our program that late October day was "A Celebration of Halloween" and, despite the fact that it included rousing selections from *Phantom of the Opera, Jekyll and Hyde,* and *Danse Macabre,* the applause each time was succinct, muted and painfully tasteful.

I began to feel guilty for wearing a vivid orange top with a keyhole neckline (brazen hussy!), as well as for pairing it with a black twirly skirt (so theatrical!), not to mention the in-the-spirit-of-the-day accessories, like a leopard belt and matching pumps (shameless show-off!).

I heard myself start to introduce each act a little more quietly than I had the one before, and, mysteriously, trade in my warm, gregarious self for a female version of Joe Friday during his weekly Dragnet monologues. Likewise, my performers were delivering the most nondescript renditions of their pieces that I'd ever heard. By the finale, I no longer recognized any of us.

Afterward, as we all trekked to the parking lot, trying to recalibrate and recapture our real personalities, a veteran piano mom summed it up perfectly: "I miss the hecklers!" she squawked.

Lesson:

There is, most definitely, such a thing as being "too polite," and its effect is not only tremendously limiting but, also, potentially frightening and curiously infectious.

49

Nursing Home No. 3: Juuuuuuust Right

Our third nursing facility was modern and grandiose, with a shiny digital black grand piano that was surrounded by dozens of rows of plush seating, arranged in a semicircle. The ceilings were high, and everything was bathed in sunlight.

I arrived forty minutes early, as I always do, to acclimate and trouble-shoot, if necessary. But this smooth-running ship was completely ready to sail, with at least a dozen residents already seated and cheerfully waiting to be entertained.

I moved ten folding chairs to one side of the piano, for the students who would be arriving soon. Immediately, a woman who'd been sitting front and center toddled her way over and plopped down on one.

"You don't want to sit there," I cautioned, with a teasing lilt to my tone, "because, when the show starts, I'll make you get up and play."

"Oh, you want me to play?" she asked, and obediently headed for the keyboard.

"Nora, no!" called one of the aides nicely. Then, to me, she explained, "She used to be a piano teacher."

Another early bird was someone I had seen in her daughter's home many years before, when I'd started teaching lessons. In fact, it was her daughter who had clued me into this brand new facility in the first place. I sat down next to her. "Hi!" I beamed. "It's so nice to see you again. Do you know that your grandchildren are performing here today?"

"My grandchildren?" she asked.

"Yes," I answered, awaiting her reaction of surprise and delight.

"I don't have any grandchildren," she said, and scoffed, making the surprise mine instead.

Mortified by such a *faux pas* (was I doing so many of these nursing home gigs that all elderly women were looking familiar now?), I said, "Oh dear; I'm so sorry. I thought you were Mrs. Johnson."

"I AM Mrs. Johnson," she admitted at once.

"Then I have news for you," I told her. "You have grandchildren, and they're going to be here today performing."

"I do?" she gasped with enthusiasm. "They are?" She turned to the woman on her right and exclaimed, "I have grandchildren! And they're going to be here today performing."

"Really?" said her neighbor, as if she were hearing this news for the first time. "Why, Josie, that's wonderful!" She turned to the woman on her right and said, "Josie's got grandchildren, and they're coming today to play the piano."

That resident, in turn, passed the news on to the woman on her right and, for the next ten minutes, I watched the re-enactment of my favorite elementary school game, "Telephone," play out before my eyes. This group was tightly knit, though, so there were no miscommunications.

When Josie's grandchildren arrived – and she recognized them immediately – the entire row lit up and clapped for them. They did likewise for every single student who performed, including the thirteen-year-old voice student who was debuting, and nervous beyond description.

She missed entrances repeatedly, short-changed beats on practically every measure, and became tragically lost several times. She forgot words and missed pitches but, to her credit, she never once stopped singing. They clapped and cheered for her as if she were Judy Garland. I could have kissed them all.

Still, though, I could see, in my debutante's eyes, the shame and humiliation I, myself, had experienced at her exact same age so many years before.

But then, after our show was over, something beautiful happened: a peppy, snazzily-dressed resident approached her and exclaimed, "You were my favorite one! You have a BEAUTIFUL voice. Don't ever stop singing. And I know what I'm talking about, too. I used to sing professionally in clubs in New York City for twenty years. You're really good, Honey! I enjoyed you very much."

And just like that, I watched the light return to my little sweetie's eyes, and knew we'd found our perfect spot to visit forevermore.

Lesson:

It's not necessary to suffer, yourself,
when you're making an effort
to enhance someone else's life.
Always hold out for your perfect match.

Two Scares and A Shiver

In all the years I've gone
into other people's homes,
on only two occasions have I ever feared for
my physical well-being.
And, in another instance,
I feared for men everywhere

50

Not Exactly Southern Hospitality

The first scare occurred at the third lesson of a student who'd just moved to town from Georgia. She was six and cute as can be, especially with that irresistible little Southern drawl. Her mom was a warm, congenial nurse with lots of Southern graciousness. The older brother was twelve and quiet, but still very charming, with that cute syntax of his, too. They seemed like a terrific new family.

The second week, a few minutes before the lesson was over, the dad arrived home, and the mom introduced us. He was medium height but with a strapping build and a very strong, aggressive handshake. He had the Good Ol' Boy charm working, but his stare was too long. He kept giving me the up-and-down when his wife engaged me in conversation with her back to him, and I felt crawly and disgusting as I left their house.

The third week, when I got out of my car and saw him waiting inside the open doorway, every hair on the back of my neck prickled. Every nerve ending, body-wide, was immediately on high alert, and my Little Voice said, "Get back in your car and race the hell away from here!"

"Hiiiiii! How y'all doin' today?" he called to me.

I swallowed down the enormous lump of fear in my throat and responded, "Great, thank you," as I walked briskly past him. I cringed as he closed the door.

"My wife and son are out of town," he said immediately. "Here, let me take your coat."

"Actually, I'm always cold," I said honestly. "I always keep my coat on during lessons. I know it's peculiar, but I truly do do that. In fact, my students are forever teasing me about it."

"Nonsense," he said, physically peeling it back from my neck and shoulders. "I'll just turn up the heat for you."

Just then, to my total relief, Savannah skipped into the room. I patted the back of my chair and said to her father, "Here, you can put my coat right here. That'll be perfect."

"Sure thing," he drawled, brushing up

against me as he did.

Throughout the course of the lesson, that horrible man walked by my chair and brushed up against me at least ten times. With one of them, I attempted to squirm out of his way, but he put his hand pseudo-comfortingly on my shoulder and drawled, "I know it's tight in through here. Sorry about that." *Ugh.*

Three times, he stopped midway up the stairs, directly above where Savannah and I sat doing our lesson, and just stared lasciviously. I pretended to be oblivious and concentrating fully on my beloved little student. What I was actually doing was grasping my pen Psycho-shower-scene style, just in case.

At the end of my thirty minutes, I deftly scooped up my coat and piano bag, as well as Savannah herself, and cavorted us merrily to the front door. "You did great today," I told her, then put her down but kept her hand playfully in mine. She shot me the cutest smile.

Never taking his eyes off me, the dad pressed the lesson fee into the palm of my free hand and closed my fingers around it with his own. "Thank you." There was such a nauseating gush to his tone. "I want to give you my business card here, too, in case you ever need to get ahold of me. It's got my private number on it right under my name and job title – Vice President of Networking."

"Oh, okay. Great," I said, not acknowledging one iota of the creepy undercurrents in which he was trying to drown me. I walked casually to my car, ever the quintessential poker player.

Once around the corner, though, I dialed my husband's number and choked out the story of what had just happened.

"Give me his number," he said, with a quiet, eery calm, and I gladly obliged.

He called him with the ruse that I was afraid my wallet had fallen out of my bag, and could he please stop over and check the area. The Vice President of Networking reverted to Good Ol' Boy hospitality at once, and warmly offered up the address.

My beloved husband arrived there in record time, and doled out his own brand of undeniable undercurrents. It started with the iron grip handshake that said, "You know there's so much more power in reserve should I need it," progressed to a dead, humorless gaze as he asked, "So, were you watching her get into the car? Do you think you would've noticed if she dropped her wallet?" and finished off with, "Well, hopefully everything will work out, and I won't have to come back here."

As sweet and warm, considerate and kind-hearted as my husband is, he also has a take-no-prisoners side to him when protecting his family. I can only imagine the impact it had on the Vice President of Networking.

I got very lucky the following Sunday night, when I called the private number on the business card to deliver the lie that, due to "scheduling conflicts that had just arisen," I was no longer able to provide lessons to Savannah. No one answered, so I got to leave word in the form of a voicemail message. But doing it that way, rather than on their home phone, meant that the Vice President of Networking was going to have to convey the message to his wife, who would wonder however in the world such number came to end up in the piano teacher's hands.

She called me during the day on Monday and asked, incredulously, "My husband gave you his business card?"

"Yes, wasn't that as lucky as life gets?" I gushed, feigning yet another stellar performance of ignorance and naiveté. "I lost my wallet last week, and so didn't have your home phone number anymore, so, if he hadn't given me that business card last week right before I left your house, I never could've gotten word to you in time about the lessons. It was so serendipitous, wasn't it?"

There was a sigh and then silence on her end of the line, and I sensed it was because she'd been down this same ugly path – and, perhaps, had needed to uproot her family because of it – far too many times already in her life. It was simply impossible not to feel extremely sad for her.

Lesson:

Whether you're in one
of the passenger cars itself, or watching
from the station,
you're still experiencing the train wreck.

51

Down in the Boondocks

The other scare from my history was less overt but, because of the location of the house, it was a far more potentially dangerous situation, and always festers in my mind as Something Bad That Was Unmistakably Possible.

The family was obviously quite wealthy. Their lavish, one-of-a-kind designer home sat in the middle of what looked like about twenty acres on a secluded private road, many miles from any other development in their upscale suburb. The sinuous driveway, easily an acre long, was completely obscured by thick evergreens on both sides. Behind the house lay a steep hill, a thick, lush valley, and a substantial developer-created body of water.

The first night I ever did a lesson there, the mom and dad were "performance friendly" to me, in light of the artist they were entertaining. He'd been commissioned by them, they explained, to create a Pollack-like triptych, each component of which was at least 36" x 60". The artist was in the process of hanging them on the slanted living room wall, just beneath the skylights.

Meanwhile, my new seven-year-old student and her three-year-old brother were in Winnie the Pooh footie pajamas. They were a nice injection of realism into this otherwise bizarre tableau.

"How about some champagne?" the dad, way over-smiling, asked.

"No, thank you," I answered politely. "Jocelyn and I are just going to get right down to work here, aren't we, Jocelyn?"

She looked up at me and nodded adorably.

"Oh, very GOOD!" he over-emphasized, as he continued to over-smile and over-gesture.

Moments later, still over-smiling, he set an enormous flute of champagne on the piano in front of me. "In case you change your mind." He gave me a conspiratorial wink and went immediately to the top of my People I Can't Stand list. Ugh and double ugh!

I've been in countless homes. When something is "off" about a family, I sense it from the moment I step across their threshold. My Little Voice told me, every time I went there, that something was very, very off in that house.

The dad was always "on": hyper-effusive, excessively congenial, always declaring any words I ever expressed as "brilliant" or "dazzling" or "absolutely delightful." He commented on my hair, my clothing, even my make-up, for heaven's sake, in an effort to remain engaged in conversation. As time went on, I wore drabber clothes, loose-fitting tops, and skirts to the middle of my calf. It mattered not even a little.

In addition, the mom was rarely around. Her family would say she was just always "out running." (Certainly understandable...)

Lesson times for this family seemed to fluctuate frequently. Yet, every time I went there, someone in the house was always either getting into or just getting out of the bathtub. Several times, Jocelyn would be extremely introverted during lessons and, no matter how many teacher tricks I tried, I could not draw her out. Twice, she even began crying hot, silent, seemingly unprovoked tears while playing a song, but insisted "nothing's wrong" when I showed concern. It was horribly unsettling.

One day, as I was getting ready to leave, Jocelyn's three-year-old brother smiled up at me and said, "You've got a pretty cute tushy there!" His father burst into peals of laughter and said, "Wow! It sure has started early with THIS one!"

Chilling as that was, however, the day that unnerved me to my core was when, because of a traffic jam, I'd arrived twenty-five minutes late to their house and found Jocelyn and her mother and brother just inside the front door, removing their coats. Seeing me, the mom looked at her husband and asked, "Oh, you never got to have a voice lesson?"

I looked from one to the other for clarification, and the mom said, "The kids hadn't wanted to leave Grandma's, so I called home and told my husband to call you and cancel the lesson. But he said he'd prefer to just keep it and have you give him a voice lesson instead."

"Oh, my, that's too bad," I lied. "That would've been fun. Actually, I have some bad news. I have some family obligations that I need to tend to, starting this week, and have to reduce my student load by a pretty big number. Unfortunately, the only fair way I could come up with to do that was to base it on seniority. So, I hope you forgive me, but this will have to be our last lesson."

Lesson:

Sometimes, you just live right in this life.

52

The Merry (Black?) Widow

When a woman called me to say she'd recently lost her husband, and wanted to try piano lessons as a way to assuage the loneliness of her days, I was happy to oblige.

She was in her mid-30's blonde, petite, extremely beautiful, stylish, warm and quite charming. Her house was elegant, and in the most affluent of neighborhoods. She was gracious, funny, enthusiastic, and a diligent worker from day one. Yet never did I find a student who unnerved me more.

She'd buried two husbands in twelve years, she told me, and made references to, and had photos of, twin toddler sons, though there was not one shred of any physical evidence of them. A portion of each lesson was spent with her regaling me with stories of men she'd recently met online or dated. A handful she'd even flown to meet in other states.

Within four months, one in Los Angeles delighted her so much that she sold her gorgeous home to live closer to him. At our last lesson, she said, "But, if it doesn't work out, at least I'll be in a place with lots more single guys than there are here."

She gave me a dazzling, satisfied smile.

I listen attentively to the trailers for *20/20* and *48 Hours* every week, imagining she could possibly be my brush with infamy.

Lesson:

It is not so much paranoid as it is wise
to remember that what's on the surface
does not necessarily reflect
what's deeper down. The most sought-after
mushrooms, after all, spring from manure,
and beautiful skyscrapers are built atop
dank basements and sewer systems.

Recital Adventures

I hold an annual voice, flute and piano recital on the Sunday closest to June 6th, in loving recognition of my father's Yahrzeit, the anniversary of his death.

No two years are ever the same, except in the fact that they are, without question, exciting – just each in its own special way.

53

A Maintenance Crew of One

I like all my metaphoric duckies in a row, so I am a world-class, super-efficient planner. Yet, far too many times, something comes up on or before the recital to let me know that I, like everyone else, am in the hands of fate.

Take, for example, the year I entered the room where the big day was to be held, only to find the floor plan skewed ninety degrees from the way I'd drawn it on the set-up sheet! With the clock ticking until people would begin arriving, I decided that, in the same amount of time it would take me to trek to the reception desk, have the maintenance guy hear the page, subsequently respond, and move each chair, I could change the whole room around myself.

Except, wait, the maintenance guy was probably brawny, and I weighed 110 pounds. No matter!

I quickly arranged the chairs without incident – no problem there. But then there was the minor detail of the grand piano. Only two legs were on casters. As I put my shoulder against the third leg, and put my arms around its substantial girth, in an attempt to raise it, I heard my back give a very definitive "POP!" which was followed, at once, by acute pain throughout my lower vertebrae and down my leg.

It took six weeks and twelve chiropractic visits before that felt better again, and it was, without question, THE longest recital of my entire career.

Lesson:

I am not Wonder Woman after all.

54

Tenacious Patron of The Senior Adult Lounge

At the JCC, where I held my early recitals, we had the luxury of a large, predominantly glassed-in, sun-drenched room called The Senior Adult Lounge, dubbed such because, during the business week, the older JCC members use it for their meetings and social clubs. On Sundays, however, they lease it to others, and it served as a perfect venue for us.

Well, except that one year.

Performing at the piano was quiet, mercurial Nathan, a lad of ten, with a hearty ADHD affliction. About two measures into his three-page piece, I glanced toward the glass door that opened onto to the second-story deck, and amused myself with what my mind tricked me into thinking it saw: a senior adult who, with her skinny, vespine body and huge post-operative sunglasses, looked like the personification of the cartoon character Maxine. In my mirage, she stood amidst the rubble of the construction project and orange mesh barriers. Another glance in that direction a moment later, though, and I realized, with incredulity, that it was no mirage! There actually was an octogenarian on the second-story balcony! Somehow, she'd scaled the orange fence on the ground below, climbed the crumbling steps on the outside of the building, and ended up on the wrong side of the Senior Adult Lounge door.

On our side of the threshold were huge, black and yellow diagonals, around an ominous sign that cautioned: WARNING! ALARM WILL SOUND! Some of the parents in the audience were now becoming aware of the interloper as well, and I knew catastrophe was on the ever-nearing horizon.

"Don't stop playing no matter what," I whispered to Nathan, the least likely child ever to ignore a distraction.

Maxine cupped her glasses, pressed her face against the door, and rattled the handle. Locked. She tried again, this time with vigor and conviction. Everyone on that side of the room was now mesmerized with the oddity before them, rather than the stellar job that wonderful Nathan was offering up after months of diligent effort.

When everyone pretended to ignore

her, she became rabid about it. A mom near the door, seeing and obeying the yellow and black warning signs, stood before Maxine and pantomimed a perfect rendition of "Go around." But that just incensed the old woman even more. She put a scrawny hand on her hip, scowled fiercely, and proceeded to pound now with two-fisted abandon.

Miraculously, my ADHD boy, God bless him, played on.

Now a JCC reception desk worker, summoned by one of the parents in the audience, dashed to the door, her knot of keys clanging loudly with each stride. But the door hadn't been opened for at least six months, the length of time the balcony had been under construction, so it was not budging. Three beefy piano dads began thrusting their collective weight against the door, while sweet Nathan played on.

With as scant an amount of attention as he was receiving for his excellent performance, he could have been playing twenty verses of "Deutschland Uber Alles." But never once did he stop, my amazing trouper.

As he stood to take his bow, the door finally gave way, and in stormed the senior to the lounge that she felt was rightfully hers. She stood directly in front of Nathan to bellow to his audience, "WHAT'S WRONG WITH YOU PEOPLE? DIDN'T YOU HEAR ME KNOCKING OUT THERE?" She then huffed out of the room, furious and disgusted with the ineptitude of everyone before her.

My little pianist gave me a quizzical look, bowed, and was acknowledged, at long last, by tumultuous applause.

Lesson:

Never underestimate the ability of a child to step up to that proverbial plate exactly when you need him to more than anything.

55

Sweet Tweets

Nearly every year at the recital, I have at least one parent/child duet, and it's always an audience favorite. One year, though, it was a grandfather/grandson flute duet, and it plucked at my heartstrings like no other.

The grandson was nine, and it was his first year playing. The grandfather, though, had attended music school and still practiced every day of his life on his rare and very valuable all-silver flute. Both had taken lessons from me during the year, independently of each other, and, in March, I posed the question to the grandson, "Bradley, so you think you might like to play flute with your grandpa at the recital?"

He gave it only a moment's thought, then said, "Sure!"

"I'll ask your grandpa this week at his lesson, too," I said. "That's only fair."

"He'll do it," Bradley said, matter-offactly. "He loves me."

At Grandpa Bert's lesson that Friday, I told him what Bradley had said, and watched him well up. "So, are you game to play a duet with your grandson at the recital?" I asked.

He looked so sad when he said, "I'm just not sure. God knows I love that boy with all my heart. The problem is that I have acute stage fright – had it all my life. It's what made me leave music school and become a CPA."

I'd had no idea of that.

"This might be the perfect chance to slay a dragon," I offered. "You've got maturity on your side now, and this is as low pressure as it gets. Plus, the audience is very friendly and claps a lot."

He smiled at me kindly.

I went on. "Think of it as a gift you'd be giving Bradley."

"Fine," he said. "Let's see what happens."

We had special two-fer lessons during Bradley's scheduled time, and, watching them work so well in tandem, and progress toward their mutual goal, was as heart-warming as life gets.

On recital day, though, Bradley came in with fear and anguish in his eyes. "I don't want to play," he told me in a desperate, overwrought tone. "I really don't want to do this."

"Well, Bradley, I never make kids play when they're feeling too afraid," I told him. "But what about your grandpa? What are we going to tell him when he gets here? Your duet won't sound as good if he plays it by himself. Plus, I think he'll be worried about you." He thought about that a good, long minute then finally said, "Okay. I'll do it for Grandpa."

"You are the nicest grandson I think I've ever met," I told him honestly.

Bert made me very nervous. He arrived with exactly one minute to spare, and looked very, very uncomfortable. "I wouldn't do this for anyone else," he admitted to me under his breath, "only Bradley."

"I am so proud of you." I squeezed his arm.

In the interest of not prolonging their agony, I bucked tradition and let theirs be the opening number. Then I handed each one a paper cup of water so they could stave off the dry mouth that can result from performance anxiety, and gave them both my warmest Proud Teacher smile.

They got through it well. The audience responded with wonderful enthusiasm. It didn't seem lost on anyone that these performers were each bestowing the gifts of bravery – and love – upon the other. It was our own personal re-enactment of O. Henry's "The Gift of the Magi."

Lesson:

Selflessness breathes life into the hearts of
not only its giver and receiver
but, also, all who witness it as well.
It leaves people changed,
in the most beautiful way, forever.

56

Senior Recitals

There is a bittersweetness that comes on recital day, with students who have continued piano lessons with me through to their Senior year. The majority have been part of my life for at least a decade, and they end up more than merely students. They become children of my heart.

It is rare that I can sit through their "swan song" and not be flooded with the memories of our times together. I watch them play, and see them as elementary schoolers – their tiny hands, their funny syntax, their enthusiasm, their Jack-o-lantern smiles. I progress to seeing them as middle schoolers: gangly, awkward, pseudo-cool despite the mouthful of hardware, brimming with false bravado. And, finally, I see them as the young adults they've become: accomplished, determined, charming and conversant, excited about what lies ahead.

They swell my heart and break it, all in the same moment, as they take their bow and then let me hug them. With a lump in my throat, I say, "I'll miss you" and, finally, "Good-bye. Please stay in touch."

I like to always bestow a hand-made gift on my graduating seniors. For some, it's a quilt for their dorm room. For others, it's a pillow on which I've painted the titles of every recital piece they ever played. For one Eagle Scout I loved, it was a candy-filled wastebasket covered with duct tape, because the boy swore it was the eighth wonder of the world.

But I also give them a book of music I know they'll love, and inscribe it with the same words my own beloved teacher wrote on the inside cover of the book she bestowed at my senior recital: "To My Dear Student (Shelley): I expect great things of you. Much love always. Xoxoxox"

Lesson:

When you let people know
you love and believe in them,
they become greatly motivated
to give you a reason.

Summer Gigs

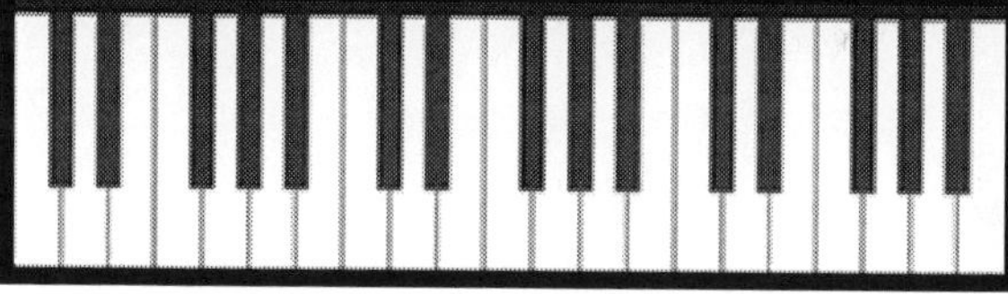

I was a tenth-grader when I learned that many of my teachers took non-teaching jobs in the summer.
I remember how unbelievable that concept seemed to me.

57

Off-Duty Teachers: Bizarro World

Our history teacher, a fleshy-faced man with a potato nose and brush cut, was talking about the project he was assigning us on The Roman Empire. "And be creative!" he honked. "I'm sick of all this bland, lifeless stuff you people are turning in these days. Take a different path than you've been taking, people! Be creative! EXPAND yourselves!"

"Looks like you've expanded yourself a LOT, Mr. Oster!" chided a smart aleck in the front row, patting his stomach.

"Teachers don't just teach, you know," Mr. Oster shot back. "We do many, many different things. Every summer, about six other teachers and I, for example, remodel people's houses around town."

Mr. Oster? On a ladder? With a hammer in his hand? Did he accessorize with a sweat-dappled, sleeveless tee shirt that stretched like Saran Wrap over that Santa Claus physique? Did it maybe not even make it over the whole protrusion, so a big slab of pale, hairy underbelly peeked out? (Obviously, Mr. Oster hadn't been addressing me as he beseeched our class to explore the creativity angle.)

"I do the framework," he expounded. "Mr. Everett, the [mad] science teacher around the corner, does all the electrical work." So, were those age spots all over his hands, or singe marks, I suddenly wondered. Mr. Oster paused and drew a deep breath. "And Mulroney does all the plumbing." Quick! Block the butt-crack image from my mind! Merciful Lord, please block the butt-crack image from my mind.

I felt just flabbergasted. There was an unwritten law that teachers did other jobs in the summer? Who knew? So it became a given, then, that when I became a teacher, I, too, expanded myself throughout the months of June, July and August.

Lesson:

If you want to wholly identify with a group,
it is incumbent upon you to participate
in the traditions they hold sacred.

58

The Best-Paying Job Ever

A friend of mine had become the board president for an inner-city nursery school. So, when summer began, I thought it would be great fun to volunteer to teach ballet, jazz and modern dance there.

I donned a shimmering, lime-green leotard and rainbow-sherbet crepe dance skirt, and signed in at the main office. It was a huge school so, by the time I finally arrived at my destination, several little four-year-old faces were peeking out at me from their doorway.

I knew this was going to be the best summer gig ever when several shouted out excitedly, "She's here!" Their classmate, a quiet little sweetie off to one side, added, with a hushed reverence, "And she's beauuuuuuti-ful!"

They all ran out into the hallway then, and gave me a group hug. It was an enchanting, life-affirming moment that I will treasure always. It was also the perfect harbinger of my wonderful three months with them.

Lesson:

Teachers are
the richest people on the planet.

59

Cleaning and Organizing

My friends have repeatedly told me that there is something intrinsically wrong with my love of cleaning and organizing anything and everything – and in record time too, no less. Yet, when they're overwhelmed with cupboards or closets or, even, entire rooms, I am the person every last one of them calls. And, when they do, I am so excited to begin the task of putting things into their proper places that I can hardly fall asleep the night before.

So, when my lifelong friend, an independent, brilliant, and super-capable woman, who can multi-task like no other human on the planet, said "uncle" in reference to a few spots in her house, I signed on for duty the first Monday following the recital.

Ordinarily, I do these cleaning and organizing gigs by myself. My friends are only too happy to go away when it's a mess and return when it's a masterpiece of ordered perfection. Not so, this friend! Like me, she views relinquishing control of anything as tantamount to lying supine in an alley with a sign dangling from her neck that reads: Pathetic and Lacking Any Social Value Whatsoever. That we're both this fiercely controlling, yet close as life gets, works only because we're the metaphorical Two Peas in a Pod. We really do see eye to eye on everything we consider substantive or sacred. The only differentiating factor, besides our looks – though we are both redheads – is that she is the quintessential sentimental saver, and I am Spartan in the area of accumulated belongings.

With the exception of my troves of family scrapbooks and students' artwork, I swear I could relinquish every other material possession I have (well, except for my flute and piano) and never flinch. My friend, on the other hand, insisted, two years earlier, during my first attempt at turning her home into a Martha Stewart masterpiece, that we must keep a lime green, one- by two-inch slip of paper with her toddler daughter's errant scrawlings on it, because said child "might want that still."

This time, though, she declared herself Truly Ready to let her possessions go en masse, to make room for the peace and satisfaction that comes with space and order.

Day One was outstanding. We cleared out, washed down, and reconfigured the contents of every last one of her kitchen drawers and cupboards. We also photographed and catalogued, for tax purposes, the contents of ten bags of cast-offs going to charities.

The glass-fronted cupboards sparkled as they displayed her newly inherited collection of antique cups. Every other nook and cranny, including the ten- by six-foot, five-shelved pantry was raised to Fussbudgets 'R' Us perfection. We spent the last thirty minutes of our time together opening and closing cupboards and drawers just to admire our achievement.

Day Two was equally phenomenal. We plowed through the master bedroom closet that is, without any exaggeration, the combined square footage of my music room and first-floor full bath. After just seven hours, we'd relegated thirty – count 'em, thirty! – lawn-and-leaf-sized bags to the garage, ready for my friend's favorite charity.

On her side of the closet, the three ten-foot-long racks of clothes were labeled "Casual," "Professional," and "Fancy." Each was put into rainbow color order. SO fabulous!

Her husband's tie collection, enough to accessorize every man, woman and child on Planet Earth, was tamed into color order, too, and displayed onto multitudinous racks for easy retrieval. Ditto for his belts and the fourteen shelves of his sweaters.

There'd even been enough time left over for me to completely clean and organize the enormous linen closet in the master bathroom. It was filled to the brim with countless sets of beautiful sheets and towels, and more hair and bath products than a Paul Mitchell outlet store.

It was a picture-perfect day, and I slept like a conquering war hero that entire night.

By day three, though, the magic had begun to fade. My beloved friend had reached her Discard Saturation Point.

We knew we had to stop when she handed me a small bag of clothes and told me to put it into a storage bag of her son's togs that we'd labeled "Memory Clothes." These were items he hadn't worn since kindergarten (by then he was in college), but which she simply couldn't donate just yet. Thinking in efficiency terms, I began removing the clothes from the smaller bag. My friend, though, insisted she had a distinct reason for wanting them in the small bag first, and then put into the bigger bag. I started to repeat her command, hoping she'd hear how ridiculous that seemed. But, instead, my officiousness incensed her, and she hissed, "Just do it because that's how I want it!"

We worked another thirty minutes or so, our peapod hearts heavy, then got into her car. At the repository where we delivered the bags, the woman responsible for providing the tax receipt put up her "Out To Lunch" sign exactly as we arrived at her vestibule, then gave us a brusque "Sorry; what can I do?" gesture with her hands.

We laughed about it all the way back to my dear friend's house, then gave the kitchen, master bedroom closet, and linen closet one last look of delight. We hugged and exchanged words of love and appreciation for a productive, bonding experience.

Lesson:

True friends understand
that we all live within our own areas
of conquerable tortures.

60

Calligraphy Lessons

The year my daughter was born, during the hours after her 2:00 a.m. feeding, she would return to sleep, but I no longer could. I spent the wee hours teaching myself several skills that have served me well throughout my life. Among them was calligraphy. So it seemed natural, then, that one May, twenty years later, when I saw an ad – "Looking for someone to teach calligraphy to a middle-aged woman in her home" – I knew I was exactly the person for the gig. Without question, it remains an expansion I will never forget.

When I called the number in the ad, the husband answered. Although I spent the full time speaking only with him, every word either of us uttered was repeated immediately afterward to his wife, the calligrapher wannabe, who seemed to be only inches from the receiver.

Me: Hi! My name is Shelley Allen, and I'm calling about your ad in the paper for a calligraphy teacher.

Husband: Oh! (To Wife) Her name is Shelley Allen, and she's calling about our ad for a calligraphy teacher. (Back to me) That's great! (To Wife) I told her that was great.

Every phone call we ever had, all summer long, was like this. Fortunately, I have a really good sense of humor, and the patience of Job. (Fortunately, I have a really good sense of humor and the patience...oh, never mind; you get the picture.)

Their house – compound, actually – was at the end of a very narrow dirt road that was almost unnoticeable, near the crest of a cul-de-sac of opulent houses. If I hadn't been advised this was the route I needed to travel, I'd have dismissed it as a foot path for the residents of the development – a short-cut somewhere, perhaps. Symbolically, just like the family itself, their home was far, far off the beaten path.

I felt not unlike Red Riding Hood as I followed this trail further and further into the dense woods. Somewhere along that five-mile stretch, it dawned on me that, at one time, this family had owned all the land where the twelve "track mansions" now stood. And, obviously, they still owned all the acres and acres from the dirt path back.

The home itself was a log cabin – but certainly not the Abe Lincoln variety by any stretch of the imagination. It was ten-thousand square feet if it was an inch, and it was surrounded by eight tiny log cabins. These were more like Abe's. Each could not have been more than one room – and not even a large room, at that.

I pulled up to the side of the wraparound porch, in between a brand new, gleaming black Mercedes sedan and a flashy, top-of-the-line Jeep Cherokee. As I got out of my car, I heard a rustling to my left, and saw a large, elevated cage housing a dog-like creature that made not one sound. It just stared at me, eerily, with very close-set, molten eyes. From my Internet research, I later learned that it was a Dingo!

Just then, a second gleaming black Mercedes sedan pulled up, and a ruddy-faced man with coarse puffs of hair on the bottom third of his head sprang out of the car. He dashed to the passenger's side, where he quickly opened the door and helped someone out.

Like him, she was probably almost sixty, but age was not going to take her without a fight. Judging from the man's obsequiousness, the funding for the battle was exclusively hers, and had been for generations.

Her hair was waist-length, and multitudinous shades of perfectly highlighted blonde, pulled into a thick, flawless braid that draped provocatively over her left shoulder and down her front. She was wearing a size two designer sundress of peek-a-boo black crepe, the torso of which would enable me, if subpoenaed, to testify under oath that she was also wearing a black lace-and-satin push-up bra. The finishing-touch accessories were a designer black leather satchel and matching stilettos. Let me repeat: the woman was crowding sixty.

Following behind her, like a good dog, the husband apologized to me for being late. The blonde vixen walked wordlessly into her upgraded Ponderosa. Once inside, I surreptitiously noted that the floors and stairways on all three levels were marble, and every piece of furniture was a show-stopping antique. The entirety of each level was completely visible from the entryway. But rather than actual rooms, there were individualized "areas" created by fabulously unique and artistically positioned groupings of spectacular furniture.

A heavy-set woman in an aqua-colored uniform and starched white apron lumbered by with an armload of laundry.

"Ask her whose those are," The Braided One commanded.

"Um, my wife would like to know whose those are," said the man.

"Twenty-three's," the servant answered.

"Twenty-three's," the man advised his wife.

Obviously, someone had slipped a hallucinogen into my box of Tic Tacs,

"Has she done Eighteen's yet?" she asked.

"Have you done Eighteen's yet?" he repeated to the laundry drone, as I bit the inside of my lip really hard just to see if it could help me wake up.

Nope. Obvious mental breakdown in front of strangers still going strong.

"Doesn't Fourteen have a lesson at the club soon?" asked The Omnipotent Despot.

"Um, yes, I believe she does," said her administrative spousal assistant. "But let me just double-check that." He quickly unzipped a large black alligator binder and slid a Vienna sausage finger down the page. "Yes, tennis at one p.m. at the club," he confirmed. "And it says here that Twenty-one will be driving her."

"Well, has Fourteen been given lunch yet?" The Grand Inquisitor asked.

"Hilde," called the husband to the woman five feet away. (Her uniform was yellow, with a starched white apron.) "Has Fourteen been given lunch yet? She has a tennis lesson at the club at one." He turned to his wife and said, "I told Hilde that Fourteen has a tennis lesson at the club at one."

The yellow servant faced her master and said, with a thick German accent, "Yes, I gave Fourteen her lunch."

"I'm going upstairs to the writing desk now," my calligraphy student advised her handler.

"Should she follow you up?" he inquired.

"Yes," she said, "tell her to follow me up."

"My wife wants you to follow her up to the writing desk," he said. He smiled and stretched out an arm in the direction of the stairs.

"Oh, very good," said I with a warm, pleasant smile to indicate that not for one second had it seemed to me as if they were all The Munsters while I was Cousin Marilyn.

Incredibly, at the writing desk, everything instantly changed. I was no longer invisible, nor was I addressed through an intermediary. This same woman who'd been as odd and off-putting as anyone I'd ever met suddenly explained everything.

"We have eight children," she said,

eyes warm now, smiling with abandon. "It probably seems a little quirky but, rather than using their names, we just refer to them by their ages." She suppressed a girlish giggle. "They live in those houses outside. Anyway, I bought these eight journals, which I think are so beautiful, because I want to write down all my memories of my children. But I feel like that should be done in gorgeous calligraphy, rather than just my regular handwriting."

And, just like that, everything changed from the grainy edginess of a Boris Karloff film, to the Technicolor magic of The Emerald City. (Though I do want it on the record that at no time in the ensuing three months did I ever, even marginally, acclimate to the pet Dingo!)

Lesson:

Children are
the humanizing common denominator
of every parent in the universe.

61

The Nature Specialist

One afternoon, in late May, as I walked the corridors of the JCC's early childhood wing, I greeted the director of the pre-school summer camp as she passed me. One step beyond, she gasped, whirled around, and shouted, "Shelley!" I'd never heard her offer such warmth in my direction before. It made me instantly wary.

"You could be the nature specialist!" she exclaimed with the same kind of revelatory tone that Newton probably used the day the apple hit him.

"Pardon?" I remember saying.

"For our summer camp! I need a nature specialist, and you could be it."

"I don't know anything about nature," I squawked.

"The kids are only four years old." Her tone was now disdainful and impatient.

"Oh, well, I probably know more than

they do," I conceded, and followed her into the office for my copy of the syllabus.

The first week, my assigned theme was "storms." I did the nursery school staple of connecting two half-empty liter-sized water bottles with the little plastic device that creates a funneled implosion. The children were mesmerized. Then, I had the teachers link arms in a back-to-back circle and run around while I wrapped them in toilet tissue until they became the camp's own personal tornado. Talk about a visual for life!

Finally, we made a ten-foot watercolor mural that we hung up and then spritzed with squirt guns. Monet-owitz! There were smiles all around from both campers and counselors. Chalk one up for the rookie nature specialist.

Week two was slated as "plants and animals," so I decided we should follow the very special path I'd discovered in the woods behind the building. "Now, remember," I said, full of excitement for our impending trek, "this adventure is for only three of your five senses: your ears, your eyes, and your nose. It's okay for your hands and your taste buds to come along, but they are not allowed to participate. No touching anything, and definitely no tasting anything. Got it?"

Everyone nodded.

I did the Jewish mommy double-check: "Are you sure?"

More nods.

I did the nursery school teacher double-check: "Raise your hand if you promise not to touch anything in the forest."

Chubby little palms filled my line of vision.

"Good. Put your hands down. Now raise your hand if you promise not to taste anything in the forest."

A second wall of little hands went up.

"Okay, then. We are ready to begin our adventure!" I chirped like a chickadee.

We trundled to the leafy inner sanctum behind the building, our pupils dilating with the substantial shadiness. We closed our eyes and listened intently for the sounds all around us, then opened them to identify the plant or creature from which they'd originated. We whispered conspiratorially, so as not to startle any of our forest friends. Then we sniffed the air to pick out the scents of pine and mint and wildflowers.

One little Y-chromosome in the group insisted that his nose was picking up the aroma of gorilla doody. Fortunately, though, his enthusiastic outburst caused a spray of birds to catapult noisily from their perches, so the potty talk was halted at once.

About ten feet from the edge of our trail, I saw the most enormous tree of all time. Dozens of thick vines snaked their way around its trunk, giving it a bit of a primordial feel.

I pointed it out to the campers but, when they followed the direction of my arm, they were immediately perplexed. They all looked back at me with quizzical gazes.

"Right there." I pointed again. "Right in front of us. See it now?"

Again they followed my extended arm. Again, they gave me the deer-in-the-headlights look.

Suddenly, it dawned on me: the trunk was so wide that all they thought they were seeing was a wall of vines! They needed a comparative-size visual. "Stay here with your counselors and watch a minute," I told them. "You're not going to believe what you're about to see!"

Like a gazelle, I loped through the fronds and underbrush until I reached the mighty oak. "Just look!" I shouted in my Enthusiastic Teacher Voice. I stretched my long, sleeveless wings like an eagle as I sturdied my spine against the massive tree. "This is just a part of the whole trunk! I'm going to put my scrunchie here in these vines so you can remember where I started."

Keeping my eagle wings outstretched to their fullest potential, I did an animated, silly-faced wiggle dance as I inched my bare neck, arms and shoulders along every last millimeter of that impressive trunk. When I finally arrived at the other side, the campers were simply agape. As they stood there with bug-eyed wonder at just how enormous that tree was, my Little Voice shouted, "Success again, Miss Rookie Nature Specialist!" I beamed.

The itching began that weekend while I was having dinner with my husband on the veranda of one of our favorite restaurants. "Oooh! I think I just got bitten by something," I yelped. But nine days and seventy-five ever-burgeoning lesions later, I begrudgingly conceded to him that he might just be right. Perhaps these weren't really bug bites after all.

I was put on a twenty-one-day course of steroids, and relieved of my duties as nature specialist by the camp director, because my fuchsia-colored toad skin was "just too frightening for the campers," and "the parents don't feel comfortable with a nature specialist who's covered with poison ivy."

Lesson:

It is only the metaphoric paths in life
that one doesn't necessarily need
to always follow. Those in forests
you have to stay on at all times.
No exceptions.

Act Three

Teaching Future Teachers To Teach

62

The Teaching Students

Beginning in 2005, I instituted a "teaching students" program. I chose patient, determined girls with sweet dispositions and good communication skills, and trained them in the fine art of teaching. It made for quite the lucrative high school career for them, and it helped me as well. Rather than having to tell prospective students' parents that I'd have to put them on a waiting list, their children were able to have lessons immediately – and at the reduced Teaching Student rate. Whenever a Teaching Student graduated, I would "inherit" her roster of students, so there was no disruption in the flow of their students' musical education.

While they were with their Teaching Students, I referred to these musicians as my "grandstudents."

I had heard a rabbi, a brand new grandpa at the time, once say, "If Abraham had had to sacrifice his grandson rather than his son, all of history would be different." Because of my grandstudents, I knew exactly what he meant.

While certainly I would never say so, on recital day, I heard every last one of my own students' missed cut-offs, each wrong note, every mis-accented *appoggiatura.* Yet I found all ten of my grandstudents to have presented error-free forays into musical genius. They were nothing short of Mozart, every last one of them.

Why my students, these prodigies' teachers, sheepishly said to me afterward, "Honestly, they played so much better at their lesson than they did here today," I have no idea. I thought they did a flawless job, and told them so afterward with great gusto and enthusiasm.

Lesson:

Responsibility with one step removed
is a beautiful commodity indeed!

63

Athletic Endeavors

One of my piano moms felt she owed me big. She was the principal at a private school and, one night, when I was at her house, teaching the last lesson of my day to her teenagers, she received a call from a teacher in her school. She rushed into the living room, ashen, and said, "Would you possibly be able to substitute teach tomorrow for the chemistry and biology teacher? Her mother just died, and she needs to leave town."

"Chemistry and biology?" I gulped.

"She's extremely organized," she rushed in. "She always writes her lesson plans out on the board in the afternoon, before she leaves. They're neat and perfect. You'll be able to totally follow them."

I looked at her playfully and repeated, "Biology and chemistry."

"Please," she implored me. "It's 9:30 at night. I was on my way up to bed. If you say 'yes' right now, I don't have to worry one more minute about this. I can just go upstairs and sleep like a baby and know that everything will be in capable hands tomorrow."

"Oh, you are such a schmoozer!" I laughed at her. "But I could use a little adventure, so, sure."

As subbing gigs go, it really was uneventful. The teacher's lesson plan was, indeed, perfect. The subjects that needed to be taught that day were "mitosis" and "the elements tables," both of which, somehow, miraculously, I did still remember from my own middle school years. The kids, in turn, were so unbelievably well-behaved that I never once had to use my No Nonsense Teacher Voice, a tool no substitute teacher should ever be without.

But the piano mom/principal never forgot what she perceived as my rescue mission. She rewarded me handsomely the following year by recommending me to a former colleague of hers, at one of our nearby community colleges, who was looking for an adjunct professor to teach a course called "Rhythm and Movement Concepts." It sounded like a music course or even, possibly, dance, but it turned out to be a phys ed course designed for students who planned to become phys ed teachers.

The room filled with brawny, muscled athletes – football players, swimmers, lacrosse goalies, and baseball pitchers. At 8:00 in the morning, they were not exactly thrilled to be there. They were even less enthusiastic when I dropped the bomb that the door would be closed and locked at exactly 8:00 a.m. each morning. Two absences would drop their average a full letter grade, and three would garner an automatic F. That part was school policy; I was merely the messenger.

We began each class, even the very first one, with four warm-up laps and ten student-led calisthenics. Enthusiasm was not exactly in abundance just yet. Rather, perpetual moaning and groaning drowned it out big time. But I forged on, undaunted. These were potential educators I had before me, a responsibility I took very, very seriously. I had only twenty weeks to get them to soak up the auspiciousness of that magic and responsibility, too.

"Raise your hand if you intend to be a lousy teacher." I offered this up as soon as our first day's round of calisthenics was completed, and we sat in a circle on the gym floor. Thankfully, there were no rabble-rousers in the group – the one upside, no doubt, to their being semi-comatose.

"Now, raise your hand if you've ever had a lousy teacher," I said.

Every single student had one hand in the air.

They looked around, smirked at each other, and nodded omnisciently. "As you come into this class for the next twenty weeks," I scanned the room with a penetrating gaze, "I want you to keep something very important in mind: those lousy teachers you've had? I guarantee that, just like you, they also never, for one minute, intended to be lousy teachers either. But, somewhere along the way, they changed. They lost their focus, they lost their compassion and, most of all, they lost their magic. This job is too, too important. You cannot ever let yourselves become like those teachers. So, every day, I want you to compare yourselves to them before you fall asleep, and never end up that way too."

I looked around and saw that their sleepy-eyed apathy had finally left the room. At long last, they were plugged in.

This first semester incorporated how rhythm and movement were not only music and dance fundamentals but, also, the basis for athletic and, even, teaching prowess. It was my job to instill that time is, indeed, everything in this world.

Being consummate athletes, one and all,

they took to the physical challenges with finesse and aplomb. Watching the football and basketball players, with their plank-sized feet, "tinikle" – first create and then perform combinations of repeated movements nimbly between bamboo poles that were being opened and closed to an unchanging rhythm pattern – was very impressive, indeed. Their test performances, however, weren't nearly as great. At each unit's end, I kept having my hopes for what I considered progress dashed.

For example, on the "rhythm" unit test, one of my top five students in the class gave this as his definition of what rhythm is: "Rhythm is a way for someone to find where someone else is, and join together to find other friends. Once they do that, they can have a party and enjoy some music."

Like, HUH?

I wrote into the margin of his paper, "I think you've confused 'rhythm' with 'smoke signals.'"

If I'd graphed the week-to-week relationship between skills I perceived my students had achieved, with those their test scores actually verified, the result would have looked like an EKG reading. I sought out the head of the department, and she assured me that what I was experiencing was typical.

"If you were teaching this exact same course to English majors," she explained, "you'd still end up with that 'heartbeat' graph, but the physical acquisition part would be low, and the cognitive would reflect the spike."

Ah, the voice of reason, common sense and, best of all, encouragement!

Plus, the projects began to give me some hope that I was getting through about the importance of not underachieving. Percussive instruments seemed to stimulate my class's best creative efforts of all.

The assignment was to design and create a percussive instrument – anything that would make a sound when shaken, struck, squeezed or plucked – and then explain to the class how it was made and how it worked.

The students voted on the completed projects, and the runners-up included:

(A) A castanet-like creation made with cork-and-plastic beverage coasters, hot-glued to tuna can lids, and then decorated wildly with acrylic paints and glitter.

(B) A theme and variation of a gong set, comprised of various sizes of aluminum pie tins, thumb-tacked onto a dry-erase board, to be struck with dowels tipped with styrofoam balls covered in sandpaper.

(C) A bowling glove festooned elaborately with tiny, colorful metal bells that jingled when shaken, and clinked when struck with chopsticks.

Everyone's favorite by far, though – the uncontested winner by a landslide – was a Snoopy-looking creature made by placing a paint brush between the open ends of two styrofoam coffee cups filled with dried kidney beans. It was all then wrapped with athletic tape. Eyes, ears, and charismatic splotches were then artistically added with black permanent marker, as were the words, "Shake my top, spank my bottom; I'm your percussive puppy." Not exactly elementary school fare but, for all of us in the viewing audience, it was, indeed, exceptional...and encouraging.

I also began to feel hopeful about the semester's learning curve when I started receiving the assessments back from my students regarding their classroom observations. They were required to visit three very different school settings of their choice within the district, and then turn their evaluations of those experiences in to me. Among the questions I included on these forms were:

(A) Did you feel the classroom you observed was run effectively? Why or why not?

(B) What did you observe that you will someday incorporate into your own lesson plan? Why?

(C) What did you see in this classroom that you will never allow when you are a teacher?

These came back to me with great thought and depth. Even the vocabulary, grammar and punctuation were improving a bit. Just as the world outside was coming to life with the rituals of springtime, my student teachers were burgeoning, too. What a great career I had chosen for myself! What delight to see such growth bursting forth!

But then came the last four weeks of class, when my athletes began taking on the role of teacher themselves, by presenting their individualized teaching practicums to the class. It was a requirement worth forty percent of their overall semester grade.

They'd received their assignments by randomly pulling out one slice of paper from two different envelopes: "Subject to Be Taught" and "Age Group." The subjects they would be teaching were the exact same ones I'd taught them throughout the previous sixteen weeks – making percussive instruments, inventing games, acquiring Double Dutch jump rope techniques, learning rhythm and movement concepts, even tinikling.

Were it not for the state-mandated videos I made of these presentations, all of which I still have in my possession, and pull out during those extra-difficult times that require serious jolts of hilarity to save the day, I would swear they couldn't possibly have been as absurd as my memory recalls. But they were. In fact, they're even worse! My memory has mitigated several of them, no doubt out of deference to my psyche... because surely these could not be the final products after twenty weeks of my tutelage.

I knew it was going to be bad when the first student scheduled kept referring to the bamboo pole-jumping techniques he was preparing to teach us as "tinkling." His classmates, now acting in the capacity of his students, giggled each and every time he said it. But he remained undaunted. The age group he'd gotten in the lottery was "elementary schoolers," so he thought it was appropriate to keep addressing us as "kiddies." That, linked with "tinkling," made it tough for everyone – yes, myself included – to take him quite seriously and exhibit our best classroom behavior. When he ended with, "So there you have it, kiddies! Now you should all be able to go home tonight and show your mommy and daddy just how great you can tinkle," every last one of us lost it.

Next came LaSalle, who'd picked "Inventing a Game and Teaching it to the Class" as his practicum, and "elementary schoolers" as his age group. He began by introducing himself, a very good start. He went on to age-appropriate warm-ups and calisthenics – also good. He then took out one of the bamboo tinikling poles and announced, "Okay, children. We're gonna play a game here I made up myself. Please get in a big circle around me."

We did as instructed, and he went on. "Okay, now I call this game 'Jump the Knife.'" We gaped at him. He continued. "Now, we're gonna pretend this stick is a great big, giant knife. I'm gonna stand here, in the middle of the circle, and swing it low or swing it high. You all have gotta jump outta the way of it, or else duck outta the way of it, 'cause if I hit any part of you with it – your head, your face, your belly, your feet – any part at all, you're out."

Yet, unbelievable as it may seem, LaSalle's presentation was stellar compared to the next practicum.

Daryl had picked "Teaching 6/8 Time" as his practicum, and "pre-schoolers" as his age group. For you non-musicians out there (and Daryl, you, too, if you're reading this, dude), 6/8 time is like a waltzing beat – ONE, two, three; ONE, two three – but it simply contains six counts instead of three. ONE two three, FOUR, five, six; not exactly rocket science.

Daryl's practicum for it was like being Alice in Wonderland right after she drops down the rabbit hole. He started us off (his pre-schoolers, keep in mind) by instructing that we needed to get into four lines with six kids in each. Everyone else in the world realizes that, in an actual pre-school class, this would have taken up the entire allotted time and STILL not have produced the intended results.

But we pretended we were brilliant pre-schoolers, and followed his directions. Then he told us to get on the little skateboards, one at a time, and race to where he'd set up orange cones, because that was where there would be a little carton of milk and a cookie the size of Saturn waiting. Each pre-schooler should then gobble down the cookie and swill down the entire carton of milk – straw not included – as fast as possible, and then ride the scooter – on our stomachs, no less – back to the next pre-schooler in line, who would then replicate what his or her predecessor had just done.

Where does one even begin to enumerate the way this whole idea was a nightmare? Plus, then there was that added little niggling concern I had about whatever in the world all this had to do with 6/8 time. But fear not, Professor Allen. All is right with the student teaching world.

In the last forty seconds of his forty-minute practicum, Daryl said, "Okay, everyone! Tell me how many kids you have in each of your lines."

We dutifully counted, and chorused, "Six!"

"That's right!" he exclaimed. "Now, when I point to your group, I want you to clap your hands eight times in a row. Okay, ready?"

All at once, I truly understood the term "tossing my cookies."

On the very last day of class, we sat in a circle on the gym floor one final time.

I asked each of my students to share the story of their lousiest teacher. Although they were all horrible, the one that left every one of us there utterly stunned was told by the quietest, most studious boy in the room:

"I was in third grade, and in gym class, and our gym teacher said it was time to do sit-ups. One girl was really fat, and she was having a lot of trouble doing them. So our gym teacher went over to her and grabbed her hair and pulled her up and down until he counted up to twenty. She was crying for the rest of the day."

I let the room stay deadly quiet for a full minute before I spoke.

"This memory is now over a dozen years old," I said softly. "Yet look how vivid it is, and how it's impacted everyone here. When you are a teacher, every single thing you do matters, and will be remembered by someone. Be sure you're remembered for good things your whole career long."

Lesson:

Authority figures of every kind have an
extremely important role in this world.
What you say and do,
and how you make people feel, matters.
Never miss a chance to tell this
to all the children in your life
because, someday, God willing,
they will grow up to be authority figures
themselves.

Finale and Encore

For me, what's made my career so wonderful is that I have never had a full-out, in-the-tank, totally bad day. Ever.

The first year I began teaching, I felt delighted almost daily by quite amusing things the students said. I knew, if I didn't write them down, they'd be treasures lost forever.

Now, thirty years later, I have a trove of little notebooks filled, cover-to-cover, with these quotes. If a day ever begins to get tough, I simply seek out any of these treasures, read through a few pages, and voilà! Instant Good Day!

Here are a few of my all-time favorites, so you can see what I'm talking about:

Lizzie (9): Know what I've noticed? As people get taller, their sense of humor gets shorter.

Clare (7): Pretty soon, it will be time to start learning Christmas songs!

Shelley: Well, first, though, we can learn some Thanksgiving ones.

Clare: Like what?

Shelley: Like "Simple Gifts" or "The Pilgrim's Chorus."

Clare: Oh! And what about "TURKish March?"

Kevin (10): [to his mother, as he's coming down the stairs from his room in the morning] Mom, did you say clean socks *and* clean underwear?

Annemarie (10): Ready?

Shelley: Yeah. Actually, I've BEEN ready.

Annemarie: No, I was talking to my head.

James (7): Wouldn't it be cool if – well, actually, it would be a little sad, too – but wouldn't it be cool if that momma bird right there fell out of the tree and died, and then I'd keep the eggs warm until they hatched, and raise them up to be real robins?

Callie (6): What's "Tempo di Valse" mean?

Shelley: I bet you can guess it if you pronounce the "V" like a "W."

Callie: [furrowing her brow] Tempo di Walrus?

Evan (7): My mom bought me fancy clothes for the recital. I have nice white pants, a blue button-down shirt, and a dark blue jacket that makes me look like the president!

Stephanie (8): Too bad piano tuners can't tune people, too.

Raymond (8): When Bach originally did "Symphony No. 9," it was called "Oyful Joyful," which roughly translates to "Ode to Joy."

Angela (9): [reading the composer line on the song she was about to play] "Franz Schubert, 1797 - 1828." Hey, why's his phone number in here?

Shelley to Lindsey (8): Lindsey, Sweetie, you have to slow down. This piece doesn't go so fast.

Lindsey: What do you mean? But it's called "Canon" – you know, like, BOOOOOM?

Sean (6): I'm going to give the candy that I get today for doing good work at piano lessons to this kid I've been sitting with on the bus, because I told him I would. So then, tomorrow, I'm gonna sit with my real friends.

Annie (7): Shelley, when I sit next to you on the piano bench, I feel love.

Right back atcha, Sweetie; and then multiplied by thirty years and hundreds of students.

Lesson:

If you love it, it isn't work.

Gallery

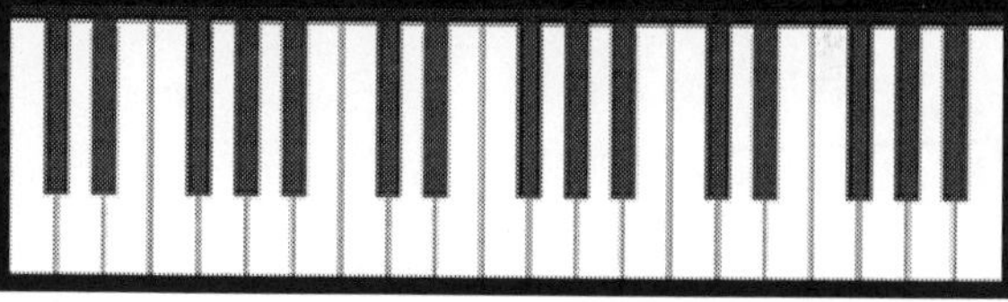

Ann Blauvelt and I

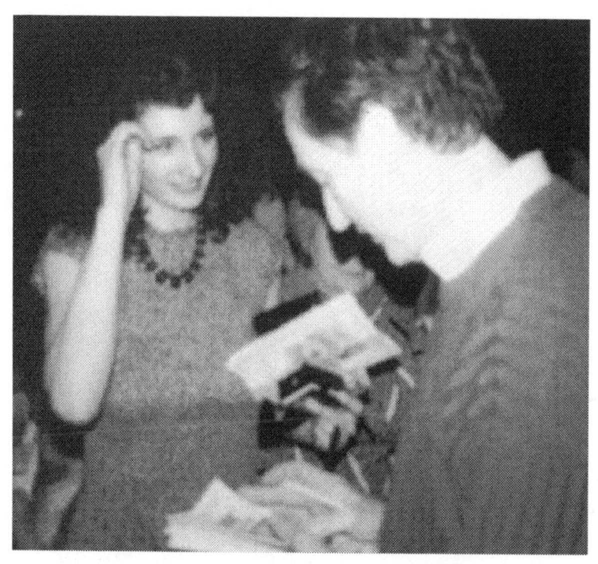

With Bob McGrath of Sesame Street after choreographing his Rochester show

A few of the Teaching Students

First Recital

Last Recital

Thirtieth Recital

The Teaching Students
—now adults in their 20's—
who honored me
by returning home
so we could perform duets
together

Layna Gray

Tamara Khalil

Madeline Couch

And this girl,
Deborah Shamaskin Trimble,
was one of my original fifteen students,
thirty years ago, and she honored me
with a duet, as well.

Her seven-year-old daughter, Averie,
now takes piano lessons with me!

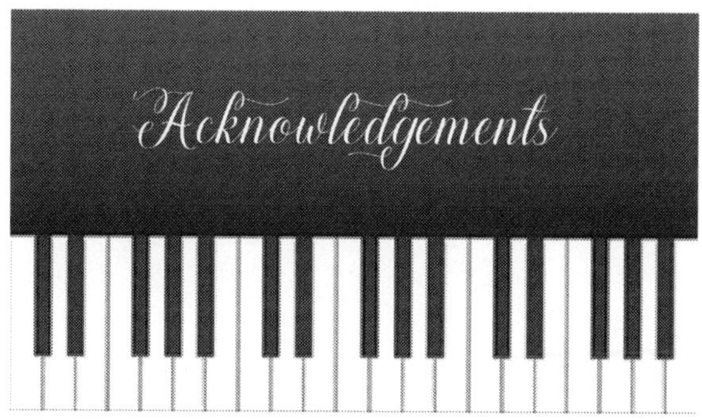

First and foremost, my heartfelt thanks to Phyllis Kasdin, who provided me with one opportunity after another to be part of her creative endeavors.

Next, my eternal gratitude to the late Lou Fisher, my writing professor and mentor, who said that this book had a universal appeal and should be published.

Thanks, beyond words, to my beloved mentor and role model, Ann Blauvelt, who was the inspiration for this book and who generously agreed to pen the Foreword. You mean everything to me, and I love you with all my heart.

Enormous thanks to my editors, Laurie Couch, Rama Davi, Michele Harber, and Jackie Rubenstein, who were as encouraging and supportive as they were meticulous at their craft, nipping and tucking my many drafts until we could all be proud of the finished product. Special thanks, love, and appreciation to Jess Williams, who lent his journalistic expertise in order to perfect the final copy.

Much love and adulation to my friend, the mega-talented writer, Sandra Stoner Mitchell, who was always an inspiration and encourager to me; to David Pascal, for his expertise in making this lifelong dream a reality by getting it to press and creating its gorgeous cover design; to my lifelong friend, Steve Richards, who came through in a big way at crunch time, and to my sweet Bobby Allen, support system extraordinaire and world's best husband, no close seconds.

I'd also like to thank all the following students who entrusted me with their musical and terpsichoreal educations: Nadia Adams, Veronica Adams, Janet Algase , Brook Allen, Derek Allen, Melissa Allen, Noah Allen, Claire Anvelt, Jenna Anvelt, Michael Anvelt, Kaiva Anzalone, Laila Anzelone, Jake Ark, Megan Ark, Clay Arnold, Michelle Arnold, Val Arnold, Alex Ballatori, Rachel Ballatori, Sarah Ballatori, Audrey Barg, Ellery Barg, Matthew Barry, Genny Bauso, Maddie Bauso, Alex Becker, Katie Becker,

Lauren Becker, Stephanie Becker, Victoria Becker, Justin Behrend, Maria Behrend, Maya Behrend, Zachary Behrend, Etan Bennett, Oren Bennett, Becca Berent, Jenna Berent, Gale Berger, Meredith Berger, Abbey Berns, Marley Berns, Grace Bernunzio, Allie Best, Bella Best, Brianna Best, Elise Black, Alex Bothner, Sarah Bothner, Genny Braggs, Rebecca Braggs, Helen Branch, Linnea Braun, Makenna Brown, Eila Britton, Anne Brodie, Claire Brodie, Colin Brodie, Fiona Brodie, Gretchen Brooker, Kate Brooker, Rebecca Buchman, Bob Burgdorf, John Burgdorf, Julia Burgdorf, Fiona Burtner, Rowan Burtner, Stella Burtner, Alexandra Camelio, Linda Champion, Zoe Chodak, Elise Coco, Stephanie Coco, Carly Cody, Annemarie Cook, Joe Coons, Sam Coons, Thomas Coons, Asher Costanza, Ben Costanze. *Kate Costanza, Maya Costanza, Audrey Couch, *Madeline Couch, Katie Cox, Sadie Craig, Annie Crane, Mary Crane, Faith Cretella, Erin Curtin, Allison Curtin, Meeta Dahake, Harper Davis, Penn Davis, Isabel DeAngelo, Matthew DeAngelo, Peter DeAngelo, Thomas DeAngelo, Catherine Dollinger, Eliza Donnelly, *Caroline Dugan, Kevin Dugan, Mike Dugan, Cassidy Dziorny, Shannon Dzirony, Janelle Eckl, Sandy Eller, Adam Eshenaur, Angelina Fantigrossi, Gwen

** Teaching Students*

Faulkner, Allie Federoff, Darcy Fergerson, Marlee Finestone, Sam Friedman, Charlie Fyles, Josie Fyles, Alexandra Gabay, Julia Gamet, Owen Gamet, Addisyn Gangai, Aidan Gangai, Jonah Garroway, Jenna Geary, Hannah Geller, Sarah Geller, Cindi Giffin, Allessandro Giorlami, Nathan Gittleman, Katie Golini, Nicky Golini, Sam Golini, Bonnie Grabel, Marissa Grammar, *Layna Gray, Sydney Gray, Taylor Gray, Jonathan Grode, Cara Guth, Noah Guarnera, Jenna Hackett, John Hackett, Lilly Hajec, Jack Halstead, Nick Halstead, Alex Harding, Robbie Harding, Grace Hanrahan, Jane Hanrahan, John Hanrahan, Katy Hanrahan, Marty Hanrahan, Ahuva Hanau, Rachel Hanau, Shira Hanau, Beth Harris, Alyson Herlehy, Rebecca Hermann, Catalina Hess, Ethan Hess, Amy Hildreth, Nancy Hildreth, Ronnie Hollenberg, Eli Horowitz, Jacob Horowitz, Sam Horowitz, Beth Hyland, Elizabeth Ingham, Roy Ingham, Sam Ingham, Erik Jensen, Kyle Jensen, Keyome Johnson, Daniel Johnston, Catherine Jordan, Emme Jordan, James Jordan, Juliana Jordan, Lila Julseth, Ruby Julseth, Sawyer Julseth, Addy Kalsuga, Bill Kalsuga, Kathy Kalsuga, Evie Kaproth-Joslin, Ivan Kaproth-Joslin, Tristan Kaproth-Joslin, Amy Kaplan, Sharon Kaplan, Ohad Katz, Raviv Katz, George Kavanaugh, Taylor Kavanaugh, Elizabeth (Kellner)

Passerino, Eileen Kelly, Will Kelly, David Kersh, Michele Keyser, Stephanie Keyser, Daniel Khalil, Hannah Khalil, *Laura Khalil, Mira Khalil, *Tamara Khalil, Tobi Khalil, Isabelle Khan, Norah Khan, Alex Kinel, Dana Kinel, Jonathan Kirkpatrick, Corey Kleiman, Marni Klim, Stefan Korfacher, Ty Korfmacher, Ari Kramer, Ethan Kramer, Edie Krieger, Leah Krieger, Pearl Krieger, Sarah Krieger, Sharon Krieger, Brynn Kreilich, Nicole Leute, Jessie Levit-Shore, Sarah Levit-Shore, Justin Long, Maddie Long, Harrison Lucas, Sabine Lucas, Trevor Lucas, Chris Mahar, Ellie Mahar, Kiki Mahar, John Mahar, Lena Mahar, Natalie Mankoff, Noah Mankoff, Noah Mannelli, Sonia Mannelli, Jason Markham, Sarah Markham, Aalianna Marietta, India Martin, Mark Martin, Phoebe Martin, Sam Martin, Jacob Massa, Zachary Massa, Xander Massa, Sahar Massachi, Shelly Massachi, Talia Massachi, Kevin Matthias, Norah McCormack, Andee McEvoy, Kelly McEvoy, Linda McEvoy, Tessa McEvoy, Claire McKenna, Liam McKenna, *Maggie McKenna, Owen McKenna, Liam McGuire, Libby McNabb, Marie McNabb, Payton McNabb, Ryland McNabb, Lisa Mendler, Lindsay Michaud, Samantha Michaud, Carey Middleton, Christopher Middleton, Gina Middleton, Sharon Middleton, Claire Mirsky,

** Teaching Students*

Ella Munger, Lila Munger, Elsa Murphy, Erin Murphy, Melissa Murphy, Nicole Murphy, Parker Murphy, Lisa Musa, Lubi Musa, Michael Musa, Sarah Musa, Harper Nielsen, Caitlin O'Connor, Kaden Ohora, Rachel Olin, David Olivo, Emma Olivo, Grace Olivo, Abigail O'Neill, Chloe Papier, Albert Parisi, Samantha Parisi, Allison Parker, Megan Pasquantonio, Joshua Pelusio, Olivia Pelusio, Owen Pelusio, Evan Perrilleon, Justin Perrilleon, Lilia Petrenko, Dan Pierce, Logan Pilkington, Lucy Pilkington, Hannah Pisher, Berkeley Pollack, Larkin Pollack, Lily Powell, Sam Powell, Peyton Proksch, Owen Proksch, Steven Raff, Leela Ramaraju, Reena Ramaraju, Claire Randazzese, Emma Randazzese, Sophia Randazzese, Rebecca Rauscher, Sophie Ravina, Catherine Reeder, Leah Reichman, Aaron Reisinger, Olive Reisinger, Evelyn Reynolds, Dave Rizzo, Lisa Rizzo, Olivia Rizzo, Emma Roberts, Wynn Roberts, Crystal Robinson, Ben Robboy, Carlyn Robboy, Erin Robboy, Leah Rodriguez, Rebecca Roeder, Allison Roman, Claudia Ronchetti, Judy Ronchetti, Owen Ronchetti, Will Ronchetti, Drew Rosenberg, Jared Josenberg, Talia Rosenberg, Naomi Rosen-Marx, Natalie Rosen-Marx, Emily Rubenstein, Jilliann Rucker, Joe Rucker, Ian Schaefer, Marina Scalise, *Erin Schantz,

Addie Schenkel, Colby Schenkel, Boomie Schlagman, Channah Schlagman, Sarah Schlagman, Shalom Schlagman, Julie Schneff, Ben Scheuering, Ellen Scheuering, Lucy Scheuering, Pete Scheuering, Abe Schwid, Ben Schwid, Jake Schwid, Maddie Schwid, Alissa Seidman, David Seidman, Katja Sertl, Andrea Shamaskin, Deborah Shamaskin, Sara Shamaskin, Danielle Shapira, Rachel Shapira, Jessica Sherin, Rachel Sherin, Alana Silber, Jacob Silber, Emily Silberstein, Nancy Silberstein, Scott Silberstein, Sydney Singer, Ally Sirotenko, Andrea Sirotenko, Nick Sirotenko, Shivani Singh, Katie Smolensky, Lauren Smolensky, Liana Sohn, Ava Solomou, Mia Solomou, Sophia Solomou, Patricia Somerville, Lyla Stevens, Jake Suss, Drew Taddeo, Ed Taddeo, Lizzy Taddeo, Sarah Taddeo, Will Taddeo, Maria Tarduno, Claire Templeton, Archer Tenhaeff, Christy Tenhaeff, Liesel Tenhaeff, Ally Thayer, Kaitlyn Thayer, Owen Thayer, Jack Thiemel, Michael Thiemel, Evan Thomas, Madeline Thomas, Meredith Thomas, Julia Tomanovich, Derek Torres, Eliza Torres, Trevor Torres, Averie Trimble, *Abby Tripler, Genny Tripler, Keith Tripler, Scott Tripler, Hannah Trumble, Rachel Turner, Ben Ureles, Sonia Ureles, Clara Vandeburg, Inez VanKeken, Kiki VanKeken, Addison Vernon, Debbie Vernon, Kat Vernon,

** Teaching Students*

Patrick Vernon, Kalyn Viggiani-Cole, Theo Viggiani-Cole, Susan Voce, Claire Vorrasi, Emma Vorrasi, Ethan Vorrasi, Julie Vrbancic, Ella Wade, Grace Weed, Jane Weed, Kelly Weed, Helen Whalen-Cohen, *Sarah Whalen-Cohen, Kathy Whalen, Faith Wheeler, Hope Wheeler, Jared Whitaker, Alex Whitman, Elise Whitman, Susan Wiener, Alex Williams, Charlotte Williams, Jess Williams, Kyle Williams, Massey Williams, Sasha Williams, Sammy Wilson, John Winter, Maddie Winter, Talia Wolff, Finn Wood, Simone Wood, Daniel Yelin, *Hannah Younger, Rachel Younger, Emma Zeger, Rachel Zeger, and Sarah Zeger.

** Teaching Students*

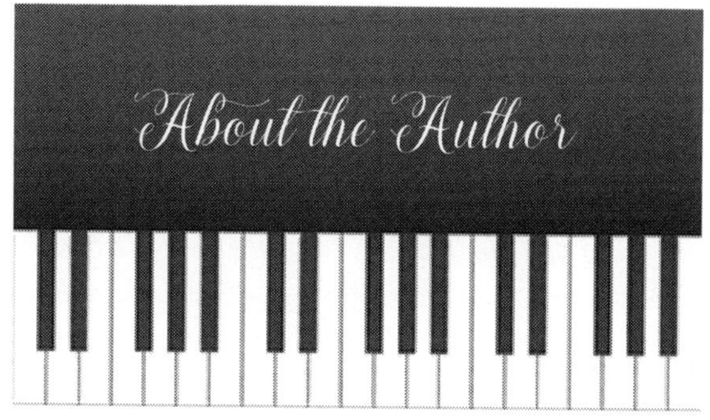

Rachelle "Shelley" Allen had been joyfully immersed in the creative and performing arts since beginning piano lessons at age five. A subsequent floutist, accompanist, dancer, opera singer, choreographer and even costume deisgner, she embraced every facet of the trade with gusto and a sense of adventure.

But, in January of 1982, in preparation for Motherhood–she and her husband would be welcoming their baby in May–Rachelle volunteered at a nursery school/kindergarten and was changed forever by the classroom's master teacher, Ann Blauvelt.

From Ann, Rachelle learned the joy of teaching and knew, by the end of her first week, that this would be her path to delight and fulfillment for all the days to come.

From 1986 - 1998, those commodities came in the form of leading students in dance classes, shows and summer performing arts camps in Brighton, New York. Then, beginning in 1992, Rachelle also began teaching private voice, flute and piano lessons to over seventy students, weekly, in their homes.

Lessons in the Key of Life is an account of these times and the lessons Shelley learned from the lessons she taught. She lives in Upstate New York with her sweet husband, Bobby.

This is her first full-length book, but she has two published short stories to her credit: "Leopard" in the April 2019 edition of the ezine WOW, Women on Writing, and "A Second Chance With Randall" in Storyteller magazine. (Volume 17, Issue 3)

Coming soon are Volumes I, II and III of her book, Noteworthy Quotes, each of which contains "100 of the best one-liners by the beloved music students of Shelley Allen." Keeping one with you at all times ensures that you won't have a totally bad, in-the-tank kind of day ever again.

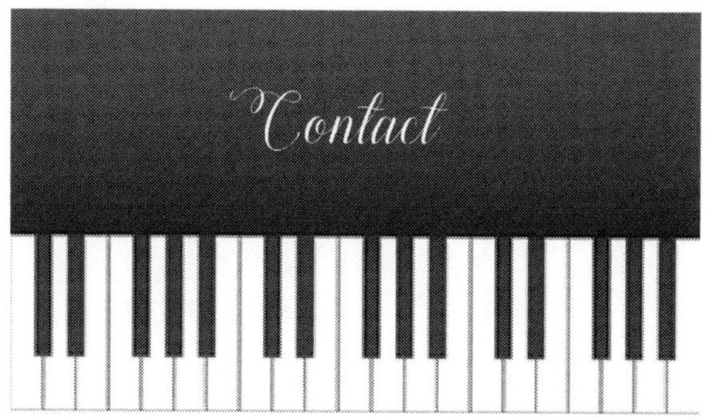

Readers may reach Rachelle Allen

at

RachelleAllenAuthor@gmail.com

and at

RachelleAllenAuthor.com